Once a Week Comprehension

BOOK FOUR

By HAYDN PERRY
Diploma in English Literature, University of London
formerly Headmaster, Merryhills School, Enfield

GINN AND COMPANY LTD

© Haydn Perry 1979

Without Answers
Eighteenth impression 1997
ISBN 0 602 22448 9

With Answers
ISBN 0 602 22497 7

Published by Ginn and Company
Prebendal House, Parson's Fee
Aylesbury, Bucks HP20 2QY

Ginn on the Internet http:\\www.ginn.co.uk

Printed in Great Britain by
Henry Ling Ltd, Dorchester, Dorset

PREFACE

This book of English tests is intended for fourth-year pupils in Primary Schools. It can be used either for testing progress and ability, or it can serve as a textbook from which pupils can work alone or with the teacher's help.

In each of the thirty tests, the first question is of the comprehension type. These questions test the reading and reasoning of the pupils. More than sixty other types of questions are included in these books. All branches of English suitable for the age group are thus adequately tested.

TO THE PUPIL

In each of the thirty tests there are five questions.

Read each question carefully, so that you understand exactly what you are asked to do before you begin.

Do not spend too long on any one question. You should answer all five questions in 45 minutes.

Make sure that you have not missed a question, or part of one.

If you find that you have made a mistake, alter your work clearly and neatly so that your teacher will know what it is you mean him to read and mark.

HAYDN PERRY

TEST 1

I. Read very carefully through the following passage, and then answer the questions.

After the Raid

When Chris awakened, the air-raid shelter was silent. Grey winter light was creeping round the door-curtain. It could have been any time. His mother was gone, and the little brown attaché case with the insurance policies and the bottle of brandy for emergencies. He could hear the milk-cart coming round the square. The all-clear must have gone.

He climbed out of the shelter scratching his head, and looked round carefully. Everything was just the same; same whistling milkman, same cart-horse. But there was too much milk on the cart and that was bad. Every extra bottle meant some family bombed-out during the night.

He trailed round to the kitchen door. His mother had the paraffin-heater on, and bread frying. It smelt safe. There were two more panes of glass out of the window. His father had blocked the gaps with cardboard from a Nestle's milk-box. The lettering on the cardboard was the right way up. His father was fussy about things like that.

Robert Westall

1. What words suggest that the **grey winter light** was a living thing?
2. **It could have been at any time.** But what time was it?
3. How do we know that the air-raid shelter was outside, and below ground level?
4. Why did Chris look round **carefully**?
5. Was his progress to the kitchen quick or slow? Choose words from this list to replace **trailed**: scampered, rushed, meandered, tore, wandered.
6. Why did the kitchen smell **safe**, and why was it warm? Who had made it so?
7. How did the extra bottles of milk on the cart show that something terrible had happened?
8. Why were the insurance policies and a bottle of brandy taken to the shelter?

4

9. What damage had been done to the house? How had it been repaired?
10. What precaution was taken so that the light from the shelter was not seen outside?
11. What did the **all-clear** mean and how were people warned that an air-raid was about to happen?
12. Choose a suitable new title from these three: (*a*) The Piping Times of Peace; (*b*) The Hazards of War; (*c*) Sleep safely in your bed, my son.

II. Change the **adjective** before each sentence into a **noun**, and use it to fill the space in that sentence.

1. **strong**   The boxer was renowned for his ——.
2. **sympathetic**   I am sure that you will have —— for me.
3. **victorious**   Finally he was proclaimed the ——.
4. **gigantic**   The Flying Fortress was a —— amongst bombers.

III. Rewrite the sentences below, filling each space with the correct word from this list: **soundly, attentively, bitterly, distinctly, stealthily.**

1. He listened —— to the discussion.
2. The thief went to work ——.
3. He slept —— the whole night through.
4. He complained —— about his misfortune.
5. So that the crowd might hear, he spoke ——.

IV. Who?

1. Who makes carvings in stone?
2. Who plans houses, churches, schools, etc.?
3. Who seeks new countries, rivers, mountains?
4. Who takes charge of the sale of goods in public?

V. Here are four **prefixes**—DIS, IM, UN, IN. Use each prefix twice to make the **opposites** of the words in the list below:

important, advantage, mortal, correct, visible, selfish, connect, practical.

TEST 2

I. Read very carefully through the following passage, and then answer the questions.

The Fisherman

There was an old man who fished alone in a skiff in the Gulf Stream and he had gone eighty-four days now without taking a fish. On the first forty days a boy had been with him. But after forty days without a fish the boy's parents had told him that the old man was now definitely and finally *salao*, which is the worst form of unlucky, and the boy had gone at their orders in another boat which caught three good fish in the first week. It made the boy sad to see the old man come in each day with his skiff empty and he always went down to help him carry either the coiled lines or the gaff and harpoon and the sail that was furled around the mast. The sail was patched with flour sacks, and furled, it looked like a flag of permanent defeat. The old man was thin and gaunt with deep wrinkles on the back of his neck.

Ernest Hemingway

1. For how long had the old man gone without a catch?
2. **Three good fish in the first week** does not seem much of a catch. Why do you think the fishermen were pleased?
3. What words tell us that the old man's luck was too bad for the boy to continue with him?
4. Why was the boy sad, although his new masters were successful?
5. How did he show that he had not forgotten the old man?
6. How do we know that the sail, like the man, was very old?
7. The story tells us that he was an old man. What words or phrases prove this to be so?
8. Find words and phrases in the story which mean: the sail looked as if the old man had really given up trying; haggard.
9. Put into your own words **the old man was definitely and finally salao.**
10. Which words or phrases describe the old man's fishing expeditions? (*a*) successful; (*b*) unfortunate; (*c*) prosperous; (*d*) triumphant; (*e*) ill-starred; (*f*) disastrous.

II. Homes

1. Who lives (*a*) on a reservation; (*b*) in a bunkhouse; (*c*) in a log cabin; (*d*) in a cell?
2. Whose official residence is (*a*) Windsor Castle; (*b*) the White House; (*c*) 10 Downing Street; (*d*) 11 Downing Street?

III. Rewrite the paragraph below, using a word from the list to fill the spaces: **hundreds, back, scarves, ground, waved, defenders, sprinted, even, goal, skywards, crossed, echoed, surprise, nodded.**

The way to the —— was open. The winger —— along. He reached the line and —— the ball. The —— were taken by ——. The centre-forward leaped ——, and —— the ball into the —— of the net. The scores were ——. —— of hats and —— were —— in the air. Shouts of joy —— round the ——.

IV. Complete the following:

Example: **boy** is to **girl** as **man** is to? (**woman**)

1. **Policeman** is to **thief** as **gamekeeper** is to ?
2. **New** is to **old** as **modern** is to ?
3. **Hyde Park** is to **London** as **Central Park** is to ?
4. **House** is to **bedroom** as **ship** is to ?

V. Jim is **small**, Alan is **smaller**, but Bob is the **smallest** of the three. In the same way, fill in the spaces in the following sentences:

1. Mary arrived **early**, June arrived ——, and Jill the **earliest**.
2. His conduct was **gracious**, his brother's **more gracious**, his sister's ——.
3. I will give you **some**, you **more**, and you —— of the sweets.
4. Jack ran **far**, Tom ran **further**, Ben ran —— along the road.

7

TEST 3

I. Read very carefully through the following passage, and then answer the questions.

The Death of Julius Caesar

On March 15th, in 44 B.C., Julius Caesar was assassinated on the steps of the Capitol in Rome. A number of rich and famous Roman senators had plotted his downfall. Some were jealous of his outstanding success as a general. Others feared that, one day, he might accept the crown of Rome which had been offered him. So his 'friends', Brutus, Cassius, Casca and others stabbed him to death on the steps where stood the statue of Pompey, thrusting their daggers again and again into the great leader, doing what his enemies in many wars had failed to do. Then they dipped their daggers into his blood and held them up for all to see.

But their success was short-lived, for Marc Antony, Caesar's true friend and admirer roused the Roman mob to seek revenge. They drove the murderers from Rome. Later, in battle they were killed. Antony and Caesar's adopted son Augustus became rulers of the Roman Empire.

1. Where did the assassination take place?
2. Why is the word **'friends'** in inverted commas?
3. What **'friends'** are named in the story? And which **true friend'**?
4. What two reasons did the plotters have for killing Caesar?
5. What did the killers show to the crowd after the murder?
6. Why did the killers choose those weapons? Why not guns of some kind?
7. How do we know that, at that time, Rome was not ruled by a King?
8. Find words or phrases in the story which mean: (*a*) murdered; (*b*) governors; (*c*) envious; (*d*) had been unsuccessful; (*e*) did not last very long; (*f*) unruly crowd; (*g*) repeatedly.
9. Choose the most suitable title for the story: (*a*) The Bonds of Harmony; (*b*) An Assemblage of Well-Wishers; (*c*) With friends like these, who needs enemies?

II. Write out these sentences, putting the **apostrophe** in its correct place.
1. Where are you? Were at Uncle Arthurs looking after the girls (plural) coats.
2. The childrens dog slept in their aunts house.
3. The ladys painting was taller than the mans.
4. The ladies sculptures were smaller than the mens.
5. The boys (plural) bicycle was faster than the girls (plural).
6. Englands goal was due to the teams efforts.

III. Change these sentences from **indirect speech** to **direct speech**.

Example: The referee said that the match was over. "The match is over," said the referee.

1. Jim asked what was the first lesson of the day.
2. The accused man cried out that he was not guilty.
3. The captain asked Tommy if he would be playing in the next game.
4. Emma suddenly shouted that she had to be home early that evening.

IV. The word **bread** is often linked with the word **butter**. Write down the words that often go with those printed below:

1. Pros and ——
2. Yea and ——
3. Crime and ——
4. Alpha and ——
5. Bricks and ——
6. Humming and ——

V. All these words begin with **KN**. What are they?

1. A sharp instrument   KN ---
2. One of King Arthur's men   KN ----
3. Soldier's leather or canvas bag KN ------
4. The joints of the fingers KN ------
5. Small hill   KN ---
6. A warning sound   KN ---

9

TEST 4

I. Read very carefully through the following passage, and then answer the questions.

The Feast at the Fjord

In the feast hall men were merry. Spruce boughs lined the walls, turning the long log shed into a forest glade. Resinous pine-boughs burned in iron wall sockets, throwing their flickering light over the many laughing faces of the shipmen and the villagers who served them with mead and corn-wine, or carried in the great wooden platters laden with barley bread and fish, or tender sucking pigs.

The smoke of the fire in the middle of the hall blew back in gusts from the high chimney-hole, for the wind was in a bad quarter. It was blowing out to the mouth of the fjord, and when that happened the smoke always seemed to come back, thick and choking, into the feast hall. But this night no one minded that, for all men spoke with great enthusiasm of the voyage they were about to make, no man knew where, in a great new ship as yet without a name.

Henry Treece

1. Of what material was the **feast hall** made? (*a*) brick; (*b*) timber; (*c*) lath and plaster.
2. Why were the walls of the hall lined with **spruce boughs**?
3. What provided the light for the feast? Why was this material chosen?
4. What word tells us that the light was not very bright or constant?
5. What two kinds of people were at the feast? Which were the hosts and which were the guests?
6. Where was the so-called fireplace? What served as a 'chimney'?
7. How do we know that these arrangements were not really satisfactory? (*a*) the fire would not stay alight; (*b*) the hall was filled with smoke; (*c*) they constantly ran out of fuel.
8. Why had the wind that night played a great part in the atmosphere inside the hall?
9. How do we know that the feasters did not take much notice of the conditions?
10. What was the reason for the feast? (*a*) to celebrate a marriage;

(*b*) to greet an important person; (*c*) because a great voyage was soon to begin.
11. Write down words from the story that tell us it took place many centuries ago.

II. Write down this passage as it should be written, in verse. Begin each line with a **capital letter**.

Sammy Smith would drink and eat from morning until night, he filled his mouth so full of meat it was a horrid sight. Indeed he ate and drank so fast, and used to stuff and cram, the name they called him by at last was Greedy, Greedy Sam.

III. Beginning with the word GRATE, and changing only one letter at a time, we can make the word BRAVO, in this way: GRATE, GRAVE, BRAVE, BRAVO. We call this a **word ladder**. Now do these:

1.	BRICK	2.	CLOWN
to deceive	-----	ornamental head-dress	-----
an instant	-----	sun-tanned	-----
copy an outline	-----	muscle	-----
	TRADE		BRAIN

IV. Below are **pairs** of sentences. Join each pair by using one of the following words: **who, whose, which, what**. You may have to rearrange and omit words in some cases:

1. The band is playing a lively tune. I like the tune very much.
2. I am able to do it. You are able to do it.
3. I have with me the witness. You can rely on his word.
4. The player seemed inspired. He scored the winning goal.

V. Complete the words below with ABLE or IBLE:

1. Can be laughed at   LAUGH----
2. Can be eaten   ED----
3. Can be reached   REACH----
4. Can be read   LEG----

TEST 5

I. Read very carefully through the following verses, and then answer the questions.

The Soldier's Dream

Our bugles sang truce, for the night-cloud had lowered,
And the sentinel stars set their watch in the sky,
And thousands had sunk on the ground, overpowered,
The weary to sleep and the wounded to die.

While reposing that night on my pallet of straw,
By the wolf-scaring faggot that guarded the slain,
At the dead of the night a sweet Vision I saw,
And thrice ere the morning I dreamt it again.

Methought, from the battlefield's dreadful array,
Far, far I had roamed on a desolate track,
'Twas Autumn, and sunshine arose on the way
To the home of my fathers that welcomed me back.

Thomas Campbell

1. **Our bugles sang truce.** Does this mean? (*a*) they played popular tunes to which the soldiers sang; (*b*) they told the soldiers that fighting was over for the night; (*c*) the buglers were merely practising.
2. What had **overpowered** the soldiers? The enemy, or fatigue?
3. According to the story, why had the fires been lit? For what other reasons might they have been lit?
4. What was it the soldier dreamed of?
5. What made the soldiers think that the stars were guards or **sentinels**?
6. How do we know that the soldier's dream had taken him to the distant land where once he had lived?
7. Which of these is true? (*a*) the soldier loved fighting; (*b*) he was only waiting for the dawn so that he could begin again; (*c*) he had had enough of the whole wretched business of war.
8. What words or phrases in the poem mean: (*a*) the sky was darkening; (*b*) exhausted; (*c*) large numbers; (*d*) rough and ready bed; (*e*) bonfire; (*f*) very late at night.

9. Consider the whole tone of the poem, especially these phrases: **our bugles sang truce, wolf-scaring faggot, pallet of straw.** Do you think it is about a present-day war, a very ancient war or a war of a few centuries ago in a foreign country? Explain your choice.

II. From the words inside the bracket, write down the **one word** that is the nearest in meaning to the word in front of the sentence.

Example: **ample**   The woman was of (slender, **broad**, slight) build.

1. **celebrity**   The man was a (nonentity, star, criminal).
2. **showy**   It was a (humble, colourful, quiet) occasion.
3. **frustration**   There was an air of (harmony, friction, togetherness) in the meeting.
4. **tranquil**   The storm passed and everything was (torrential, beauteous, peaceful) in the valley.

III. Rewrite this paragraph using a **capital letter** at the beginning of each **proper noun:**

Every day thousands of london passengers travel from piccadilly circus to knightsbridge, from oxford circus to marble arch. They are carried by london transport, by bus or by underground. Others make for the tower, st paul's, westminster abbey or hyde park.

IV. Apples, pears and peaches are all **fruit.** Write down a **group name** for each of these groups:

1. Tench, Bream, Carp, Roach, Perch.
2. No Entry, Stop, Road Narrows, Low Bridge.
3. Aluminium, platinum, gold, copper, lead.
4. Mosque, Synagogue, Kirk, Cathedral, Temple.

V. Jumbled words. Find the names of these countries:

1. ZABLIR   4. NEWSED
2. YANRWO   5. EEECRG
3. LADPON   6. DACNAA

TEST 6

I. Read very carefully through the following passage, and then answer the questions.

Trouble in the Darkness

It was the middle of the night when my Uncle woke me up and told me to climb a tree. I thought he was playing a joke on me, though he's not a person who plays jokes. In fact, he's rather a gloomy man and he thinks climbing trees is a waste of time, unless it's to pick coconuts or betel-nuts or something useful. My favourite climbing tree is a big, branching one with a thick trunk that stands near our house. (I mean, it used to stand there. I still can't get used to the idea that it's gone.)
When Uncle woke me up it was very dark and I could hear the wind blowing hard, roaring in the branches of the tree. He hurried me outside and I couldn't even see the stars, so the sky must have been covered with clouds. It seemed an odd time to be climbing trees and I started to ask questions, but Uncle told me not to argue and to get climbing.

Clive King

1. What were the boy's first thoughts when his uncle awakened him and told him to climb a tree?
2. At about what time did all this take place?
3. How does the story describe the boy's favourite climbing tree?
4. How do we know that he did not have to go far to climb it?
5. Which words tell us that the tree no longer exists?
6. How do we know that the incident took place in a foreign country?
7. Why had the stars disappeared from view?
8. Write down words or phrases in the story meaning: an extraordinary moment; a man not given to joking.
9. What was the reason for the hurried climbing of the tree? What was about to happen?
10. From these phrases choose those which the Uncle might have used: (*a*) Get a move on!; (*b*) There's lots of time!; (*c*) Start shinning up!; (*d*) Take it easy!; (*e*) No need to worry!; (*f*) Don't ask why!

11. Besides **gloomy** which of these words and phrases describe the Uncle? (*a*) matter-of-fact; (*b*) unimaginative; (*c*) practical; (*d*) a practical joker.

II. (pretty, lovely, attractive)—(ugly, beautiful, mis-shapen). Of the three words in the second bracket, **beautiful** is nearest in meaning to the words in the first bracket. Find the similar words in the following:

1. (twig, trunk, bough)—(branch, petal, stamen)
2. (willing, disposed, ready)—(disinclined, voluntary, uncommitted)
3. (active, brisk, alert)—(prompt, lazy, indolent)
4. (explicit, clear, lucid)—(incomprehensible, unintelligible, well-defined)

III. We speak of **a** tree, **a** hill, **an** egg, **an** orange. Write **a** or **an** in the spaces in the following sentences:

1. This is —— order. Write —— essay in —— hour's time.
2. I saw it in —— daily paper, not —— evening paper, nor —— weekly.
3. Would you prefer —— unpaid job, or one with —— wage?
4. He made —— offensive remark to —— ambassador.

IV. Complete these **proverbs,** or well-known sayings:

1. Fair exchange is ——.
2. Faint heart never won ——.
3. Half a loaf is better than ——.
4. Make hay while ——.

V. Write these in order of **size,** beginning with the **smallest:**

1. town, hamlet, city, metropolis, village
2. trio, quintette, solo, quartette, duo
3. quaver, semibreve, crotchet, semiquaver, minim
4. borough, town, continent, country, county

TEST 7

I. Read very carefully through the following passage, and then answer the questions.

Dantes Makes His Plans

He saw nothing, he had no knife or sharp instrument, the grating of the window was of iron and he had too often assurred himself of its solidity. His furniture consisted of a bed, a chair, a table, a pail and a jug. The bed had iron clamps, but they were screwed to the wall and it would have required a screw-driver to take them off.

Dantes had but one resource which was to break the jug and with one of the sharp fragments attack the wall. He let the jug fall on the floor and it broke in pieces. He concealed two or three of the sharpest fragments in his bed, leaving the rest on the floor. The breaking of the jug was too natural an accident to excite suspicion, and next morning the gaoler went grumblingly to fetch another, without giving himself the trouble to remove the fragments. Dantes heard joyfully the key grate in the lock as the guard departed.

Alexandre Dumas

1. Where was Dantes? (*a*) in a holiday camp; (*b*) in his dining room; (*c*) in a prison cell.
2. What was Dantes planning to do? (*a*) carve his name; (*b*) call for breakfast; (*c*) make his escape.
3. What were the iron things that Dantes could not use?
4. Why couldn't he remove the clamps from the bed?
5. Dantes needed something sharp to attack the wall. How did he finally obtain it?
6. Why didn't the gaoler suspect that Dantes had purposely broken the jug?
7. Why did the gaoler leave the fragments? (*a*) because he didn't notice them; (*b*) he wished to punish Dantes; (*c*) he did not care to trouble himself.
8. Two words are used for the portions of the jug. What are they?
9. Find words and phrases that mean: (*a*) he had frequently made certain; (*b*) there was only one thing he could do; (*c*) to make the gaoler suspicious; (*d*) went on his way.

II. Think about the word **breakfast.** It need not be **plentiful** or **expensive,** but it must be **morning.** Choose one word from the brackets that is related to the word before the bracket.

1. **Fork** (metal, prongs, stainless)
2. **Trio** (singers, conductor, three)
3. **Cycle** (wheels, chain, mudguards)
4. **Ship** (sails, keel, oars)

III. The words in each of the following sentences are in the **wrong order.** Rearrange them to make sentences. (There may be more than one answer.)

1. Filed on to the stage the orchestra.
2. Argentinian the fifteen captained by was visiting an.
3. With a cell triumph from Jim shout of bounded his
4. Pops has that song been of the Top ages for.

IV. Complete the following words, beginning with MAR:

1. Edge or border   MAR---
2. Plant with yellow flowers   MAR------
3. Animal which carries its young
   in a pouch   MAR------
4. An inhabitant of Mars   MAR----
5. One who chooses death for his beliefs   MAR---

V. The word **rifle** has more than one meaning. It means **a weapon which fires bullets** and **to rob or plunder.** Write down the words that match the following descriptions:

1. For making holes; a drink; to hit; short-legged, thick-set horse.
2. Piece of rock; inside certain fruits; a measure of weight.
3. Belonging equally to; of poor quality, or vulgar; open land.
4. Fireplace; rub to small particles, to have an irritating effect.

TEST 8

I. Read very carefully through the following passage, and then answer the questions.

A Call to Arms

The main hall of the House of Ocelot was packed with men attending a council of war. Asamodo, Commander of the Royal Guard, sat on a platform at one end of the hall with several of his senior officers beside him. Asamodo was older than most of those present, a veteran of many battles, with scars to show for it. There was a tense, expectant silence as he rose to his feet.

"Noble Knights of the Ocelot, Warriors and Members of this House," he proclaimed, "as you are aware, a new campaign of war is about to begin. I call upon you all to take up arms in the name of the King."

The men rose to their feet with a shout of acclamation that echoed from the roofs and could be heard several streets away.

Tio shouted with the rest with all the force of his lungs. He stood beside a pillar at the back of the hall where the youngest members of the House were gathered.

John Tully

1. Where was the meeting taking place?
2. What was the purpose of the meeting?
3. Who was in charge of the meeting, and what was his rank?
4. How do we know that he had served in many battles?
5. Where were the youngest members standing?
6. How do we know that it was a kingdom, not a republic?
7. How do we know that Asamodo's words were well received?
8. Write the words or phrases in the story which mean: (*a*) top-ranking officers; (*b*) one who has served for many years; (*c*) everyone was quiet, expecting something dramatic; (*d*) announced officially; (*e*) to join the army; (*f*) stood up; (*g*) a loud cry of agreement; (*h*) at the top of his voice.
9. Add the missing words: (*a*) Everyone agreed with Asamodo. No one ——. (*b*) The proposal was carried ——. Everyone voted for it.

18

II. Some words have a **similar sound** but are spelt differently.

Example: **tale, tail.** In these sentences choose the correct word from those in the brackets:

1. The victory was (holy, wholly) due to you.
2. Like (lightning, lightening) he struck again.
3. Until the whistle blew he remained (stationery, stationary).
4. What (rite, right, write) have you to judge me?

III. He and **she** are rhyming words. Write these sixteen words in pairs so that they rhyme:

mother, choir, guilt, muff, quay, plough, smother, pretty, alarms, higher, quilt, rough, calms, witty, cow, flea.

IV. Look at the word **edge.** Now look at the three words inside the bracket—(**centre, margin, middle**). The word nearest in meaning to **edge** is **margin,** so we choose that. Now do the same with these, choosing one word from inside the bracket each time:

1. **excitable**   (calm, impetuous, docile)
2. **entire**   (partial, fractional, complete)
3. **superior**   (lesser, supreme, deficient)
4. **agreement**   (discord, concord, dissension)
5. **increase**   (shrink, extend, decrease)
6. **order**   (chaos, uniformity, irregularity)

V. Choose, from the words in brackets the most suitable word to finish each line of poetry:

The glories of our blood and (birth, state, empire)
Are shadows, not substantial (events, things, happenings)
There is no armour against (luck, fortune, fate)
Death lays his icy hand on (kings, princes, queens)
Sceptre and crown must tumble (earthwards, down, over)
And in the dust be equal (ones, made)
With the poor crooked scythe and (sickle, spade)

19

TEST 9

I. Read very carefully through the following passage, and then answer the questions.

The Music-making March Family

At nine they stopped work and sang, as usual, before they went to bed. No one but Beth could get much music out of the old piano, but she had a soft way of touching the yellow keys, and making a pleasant accompaniment to the songs they sang. Meg had a voice like a flute, and she and her mother led the little choir. Amy chirped like a cricket, and Jo wandered off through the airs at her own sweet will, always coming out at the wrong place with a crotchet or a quaver that spoilt the most pensive tune.

They had always done this since they could lisp:
"Crinkle, crinkle little 'tar"
and it had become a household custom, for the mother was a born singer. The first sound in the mornings was her voice, and she went about the house singing like a lark. The last sound at night was the same cheery sound. The girls never grew too old for that familiar lullaby.

Louisa M. Alcott

1. What were the names of the four girls?
2. What did the family do before they went to bed every night?
3. Which girl was the best piano player?
4. Why were the piano keys yellow? (*a*) they were made from a yellow coloured material; (*b*) it was caused by reflection from a light; (*c*) the ivory from which they were made had grown yellow with age.
5. To what musical instrument was Meg's voice likened?
6. What had the children meant when they sang **"Crinkle, crinkle little 'tar?"**
7. Beth was **playing the accompaniment.** What does this mean?
8. What words or phrases in the story mean: (*a*) made short, sharp sounds; (*b*) just as she wished to; (*c*) something done in the house daily; (*d*) a soothing bedtime song.
9. From these, choose a suitable title for the story: (*a*) Heavens, What Cacophony!; (*b*) If Music be the Food of Love, Play On; (*c*) The Discordant Five.

10. What are **crotchets** and **quavers?**
11. Which words or phrases correctly describe the March family?
    loving, harmonious, solitary, musical, tender, jarring, selfish.

II. Fill in the spaces in the following paragraph with suitable **sound words:**

The —— of the trumpet was followed by the —— of a rifle and the —— of an explosion. An aeroplane —— overhead, and the teacups ——. The boring voice ceased to ——, the front door —— and the —— of a motor-horn meant that the spies were departing.

III.

1. Here are six **adjectives:** guilty, unseen, pleasant, practical, careful, harmonious. Choose the most suitable to go with each of these **nouns:** danger, surprise, joke, secret, preparation, voices.
2. Here are five **nouns:** fancy, business, modesty, courtesy, correspondence. Choose the most suitable to go with each of these **adjectives:** old-world, false, unfinished, passing, unanswered.

IV. Where would you expect to hear the following **phrases** used?

(a) "Number, please?"; (b) "We have lift-off!"; (c) "Have you anything to declare?"; (d) "May-day! May-day!"; (e) "Let. First service."

V. Here are some **everyday expressions.** Choose the phrase that means nearly the same as the expression.

Example: **'To look on the bright side'** means **to be optimistic.**

1. **'Wait till the clouds roll by'** means (a) shelter from the rain; (b) await patiently a suitable time; (c) work as a waiter during the wet weather.
2. **'Send someone packing'** means (a) send off some parcels; (b) tell the assistant to pack the goods; (c) dismiss someone quickly and firmly.
3. **'To take the bull by the horns'** means (a) to be a successful matador; (b) to deal with something boldly and speedily; (c) to treat something in a light hearted manner.

TEST 10

I. Read very carefully through the following verses, and then answer the questions.

I Promise You

Adown on the quay-side, adown on the quay,
A home-coming sailor once beckoned to me.
A swaggering fellow, with salt in his hair,
A glorious, roystering, devil-may-care,
A giant with whiskers, and buttons of brass,
And a great, gaudy parrot he'd bought for his lass.
"Here, messmate," he cried, "come away from your home;
Leave mother and dad and sail over the foam.
All lubbers and landsmen, just bid them farewell,
Sign on in my lugger, to where, who can tell?
Some place in the tropics where coconuts grow,
Or lands where the Eskimo lives in the snow."

Haydn Perry

1. Where did the meeting take place?
2. How did the sailor attract the other's attention? (*a*) by shouting; (*b*) by waving his hand; (*c*) by seizing him by the arm.
3. Why is the parrot described as **gaudy**?
4. The other man was not really the sailor's **messmate**. What would he have to do to become his **messmate**?
5. What does the phrase **devil-may-care** mean?
6. Find other words or phrases for: one who lives on shore; a big clumsy, stupid fellow.
7. **Sign on in my lugger.** What did he mean by that?
8. How else might the sailor have said **Sail over the foam**?
9. The sailor is described as **swaggering, roystering, devil-may-care.** Which of the following words or phrases also describe him? bragging, cringing, fawning, blowing his own trumpet, saucy, grovelling, spruce, squalid, handsome, clean-shaven, bewhiskered.

II. Which of the following is the odd man out?
1. Make it up; shake hands; continue to feud; heal the breech; let bygones be bygones.
2. Stiletto; rapier; cudgel; cutlass; dagger.
3. Arabic; Braille; Russian; Polish; Spanish.
4. Stethoscope; microscope; X-ray; theodolite; thermometer.
5. Isle; island; eyot; promontory; islet.
6. Circle; elipse; angle; arc; oval.

III. Complete the following:

Example: **Man** is to **woman** as **boy** is to ——. Answer: **girl**

1. **Fir** is to **oak** as **evergreen** is to ——.
2. **Golf** is to **course** as **ice-skating** is to ——.
3. **Either** is to **or** as **neither** is to ——.
4. **Peking** is to **China** as **Belgrade** is to ——.
5. **Shakespeare** is to **drama** as **Beethoven** is to ——.

IV. Here are some **crossword puzzle clues,** and a part of each answer:

1. A reptile	--Z---
2. A stripey, ass-like mammal	Z----
3. A test of skill	--Z---
4. A sweetmeat or confection made of sugar and ground almonds	---Z----
5. At the very top	Z-----
6. Put over an animal's head to prevent it biting	---Z--

V. Write these school lessons in **alphabetical order:**

Handiwork, Algebra, Geography, History, Zoology, Physical Education, Art, Physics, English, Chemistry, Citizenship, Religious Instruction.

TEST 11

I. Read very carefully through the following passage, and then answer the questions.

The Dance Hall

The Roxy was the last splash of light before Stradhoughton petered out and the moors took over. It was supposed to be a suburban amenity or something; at any rate its red, humming neon sign spluttered out the words "Come Dancing" six nights a week, and the grown-up daughters of the cold, new houses round about it, converged on it in their satin frocks, carrying their dance-shoes in paper bags advertising pork pies. Youths who had come from all over Stradhoughton for the catch sat around on the low brick banisters by the entrance combing their hair and jeering at each other.

I approached the place warily, along the shadows, in case Rita was among the girls who promenaded up and down the cracked concrete forecourt, waiting for their escorts to come and pay for them in. A girl I once had known was waiting by the entrance. I said "Hiya, Mavis!" boldly as I passed. She said "'Lo Billy," and I walked almost cheerfully to the pay-box.

Keith Waterhouse

1. How do we know that **The Roxy** was on the outskirts of town?
2. What is a **neon sign?** Why did this one **splutter out** the words **"Come Dancing"**?
3. Why does the writer call the houses **cold?** (*a*) because they faced away from the sun; (*b*) because they had no heating; (*c*) because the people in them were stand-offish and un-neighbourly.
4. **for the catch.** Does this mean (*a*) to do with fishing; (*b*) to find a girl; (*c*) having a ball game.
5. What seemed to be the main occupation of the onlookers?
6. Why were the girls **promenading up and down?**
7. How were the paper bags advertising pork pies?
8. Which girl was Billy trying to dodge?
9. Find words or phrases in the story which mean: (*a*) walked backwards and forwards; (*b*) those who were going to take the girls inside; (*c*) something good for the district; (*d*) with

great care.
10. Choose words and phrases that describe most of the youths outside the hall; high-spirited, aristocrats, sleazy, unkempt, rowdy, quarrelsome, genteel, posh, well-groomed, chivalrous.
11. '**Hiya, Mavis!**' ''**Lo Billy**' does not seem to get them very far. Add some remarks to carry on the conversation.

II. Complete these **word-doubles** of famous people in books:

1. Winnie the Pooh and ——
2. Romeo and ——
3. Tweedledum and ——
4. Robinson Crusoe and ——
5. Antony and ——
6. Robin Hood and ——
7. Peter Pan and ——
8. Dr. Jekyll and ——

III. Rearrange these five sentences from a story so that they appear in the correct order:

1. They stopped outside Bill's bedroom door.
2. A shapeless creature entered the room.
3. The haunting footsteps came nearer and nearer.
4. Bill flung the pillow at it and fled.
5. Slowly, very slowly, the handle turned.

IV. In the following sentences, change all the **masculine** words into **feminine** words:

Example: **He** is my **brother**. **She** is my **sister**.

1. The postmaster never saw his nephew's grandson.
2. The Boy Scouts gave a drake to the schoolboys to keep as a pet.
3. The Duke of Ruritania may never be king but his uncle might.
4. The natives thought the giant was a god.

V. **Punctuation marks** and **capital letters** have been omitted from the following sentences. Rewrite the sentences correctly:

1. oh to be in england now that aprils there said the poet
2. hampstead heath is well worth visiting on a bank holiday
3. we are about to start said the guard take your seats please
4. you are going the wrong way she snapped this is the road to dorking

TEST 12

I. Read very carefully through the following passage, and then answer the questions.

Climbing Mount Everest

June 1978 was the 25th anniversary of the climbing of Mount Everest. This great peak in the Himalayan Mountains of northern India, the highest mountain in the world, had always looked down mockingly on mere man, seeming to say "I challenge you to climb me, poor, weak mortals!" And try they did, but failed to reach the top. There were avalanches, blizzards, extreme cold, and hunger to contend with. The mountain reigned supreme; that is, until June 1953.

Then it happened! The news flashed around the world that Edmund Hillary and John Hunt had led a party of devoted climbers ever upwards until the fateful moment when Hillary himself and a Nepalese, Tensing Norgay, set foot upon the Roof of the World and looked down from a height of 8,848 metres.

What celebrations followed to mark the great exploit! Queen Elizabeth II knighted Hunt and Hillary and Tensing received the British Empire Medal.

1. If June 1978 was the 25th anniversary, when was Mount Everest climbed?
2. Where is the mountain situated?
3. Why is it called **the Roof of the World?**
4. What was the **challenge** that Everest seemed to be saying?
5. What were the perils that faced the mountaineers?
6. Who led the expedition?
7. Which men were the first to reach the summit?
8. Find words or phrases in the story that mean: (*a*) humans; (*b*) completely committed and loyal; (*c*) was always unconquered; (*d*) I dare you!
9. Queen Elizabeth II **knighted** Hunt and Hillary. What does this mean?
10. From this list choose words and phrases which describe the behaviour of the climbers: courageous, valiant, timid, spineless, brave, indomitable, chicken-hearted, lily-livered.
11. Write a News Flash or a newspaper placard announcing the

conquest of Everest.

II. There are errors in each of the following sentences. Rewrite the sentences correctly:
1. I didn't do so bad after all.
2. You are as much to blame as him.
3. He chose the larger of the three cakes.
4. Look after your pets, like I do.

III. Rewrite these sentences using **single words** instead of the phrases in heavy type:
1. He was well-known in the **streets round about him.**
2. Mr Higgs is a **hundred years old.**
3. Do the job **without wasting any more time.**
4. He is always **cheerful about the future.** His friend is **seldom cheerful about the future.**
5. His business is **drawing maps.**

IV. The opposite of **out** is **in.** Write these sentences, using the **opposite** of the word in heavy type to fill each space:
1. That land is **fertile,** but the next field is ——.
2. Tom's evidence was **factual** but Jim's was ——.
3. The customers were of two classes, **satisfied** and ——.
4. Old Jan was a **miser.** Next to him lived a ——.

V. Write in full the **abbreviations** in heavy type in these sentences:
1. He lost his **specs** in the **gym** whilst looking for a **mag,** but all ended **O.K.**
2. He was home at 10 **p.m.** from the **Prom** Concert where he heard Beethoven's **Vth.**
3. At the **T.U.C.,** the **A.E.U.** and the **T.G.W.U.** were well to the fore.
4. The **R.S.P.C.A., N.S.P.C.C.,** and **U.N.E.S.C.O.** are all well known organisations.

TEST 13

I. Read very carefully through the following passage, and then answer the questions.

In the Orchard

The garden at Les Oeillets was divided into three; first the terrace and gravelled garden round the house; then, separated by a low box hedge, the wilderness with its statues and old paths; and between the wilderness and the river, the orchard with its high walls. In the end wall a blue door led to the river bank.

The orchard seemed to us immense, and perhaps it was, for there were seven alleys of greengage trees alone; between them, even in that blazing summer, dew lay all day in the long grass. The trees were old, twisted, covered in lichen and moss, but I shall never forget the fruit. In the orchard we had not even to pick the fruit—it fell off the trees into our hands.

The greengages had a pale-blue bloom, especially in the shade, but in the shade the flesh showed amber through the clear green skin; if it were cracked the juice was doubly warm and sweet. Ever afterwards, in our family, we called that the greengage summer.

Rumer Godden

1. Into how many parts was the garden divided? Which part was nearest to the house?
2. Where did the **blue door** lead to?
3. Why do you think one part was called **the wilderness?**
4. What words are used to describe the orchard trees?
5. Why, at times, was it not necessary to **pick** the fruit?
6. The box-hedge was composed of (*a*) boxes set on end; (*b*) plants called box-trees; (*c*) palings made from wooden boxes.
7. Why did the orchard seem **immense** to the children?
8. Why did the dew lie all day on the grass, even in summer? (*a*) the gardener was constantly watering it; (*b*) there were sunshades in that part; (*c*) the sun could not reach that area of grass to evaporate the dew.
9. From this list choose words to describe the greengages: sweet, juicy, luscious, tiny, shrivelled.
10. What separated the orchard from the river?

11. What was it that formed the **bloom** on the greengages?

II. When we speak of a number of **wolves** we say a **pack**. What words should be used when speaking of the following: (The first letter is given in each case):

1. An irregular luminous band of stars. G
2. A collection of poems. A
3. A chest of cutlery for use in the home. C
4. Five hundred sheets of paper. R

III. Rewrite these sentences in **plural** form:

1. The brooch was in the woman's studio.
2. The gypsy was a prophet to his tribe.
3. The Member of Parliament sat in the library.
4. My sister-in-law liked the scarf.
5. A spoonful of that jelly for me, please.

IV. Before each sentence is a **noun**. Write the correct form of the **verb** made from that **noun** in the space in the sentence.

1. emigrant   He is going to —— to Britain.
2. satisfaction The man was hard to ——.
3. imagination He —— that he is safely home.
4. obedience   I demand that you —— me.

V. What do we call people who do the following? All the words end in **IST.**

1. stamp collecting
2. coin collecting
3. bell ringing
4. tell fortunes by 'reading' your hand.
5. tell the future from the stars.
6. keep your hands in good shape.

TEST 14

I. Read very carefully through the following passage, and then answer the questions.

Captain Flint's Treasure

We were a strange crowd as we set off to find the treasure. All but me were armed to the teeth and bearing shovels and picks, along with the pork, bread and brandy for the mid-day meal. In case I should escape, I was fastened to Long John Silver by a cord around my waist.

First we rowed our boat to the mouth of the river that ran down from Spyglass Hill. We landed and started to climb the sandy slope, to find the 'tall tree' named on the map. This would give us a compass bearing of 'N. of N.N.E.'—and the treasure.

Suddenly there came shouts from one of those who had gone on ahead. The others began to run in that direction. "He can't have found the treasure," said Morgan.

When we reached the spot we found a human skeleton with a few shreds of clothing still left on it. "He was a seaman," said one who, bolder than the others, was examining the rags of clothing.

R. L. Stevenson

1. What was the purpose of the expedition?
2. Why was Jim Hawkins unable to escape?
3. What did the party carry with them?
4. When was their meal to be eaten?
5. What was the first **mark** the treasure-seekers had to find? Where would they find this mark?
6. Explain the compass-bearing **N. of N.N.E.**
7. Why did the party break into a run?
8. What made one man prove to be **bolder than the others?** (*a*) he was bigger; (*b*) he was not afraid to go near to the skeleton; (*c*) he was forced to by the others.
9. Find words and phrases that mean: (*a*) bearing all manner of weapons; (*b*) an unusual collection of people.
10. Why do you think the hill had been named **Spyglass Hill?**
11. In the crowd of seamen, how would you immediately recognise Long John Silver? (See *Treasure Island*)

II. We often compare two things because they are alike in some particular way, though are quite different in others. For example, when we wish to say that someone is very busy we say **as busy as a bee.** These expressions are called **similes.** Choose the correct **similes** from the following:

1. as alike as (*a*) two apples; (*b*) two peas; (*c*) two nuts
2. as drunk as (*a*) a king; (*b*) a prince; (*c*) a lord
3. as safe as (*a*) houses; (*b*) castles; (*c*) schools
4. as old as (*a*) the city; (*b*) the hills; (*c*) the mountains
5. as light as (*a*) a snowflake; (*b*) a feather; (*c*) a rain drop.

III. Here are two words SAND and CASTLE. From these we can make the **compound word** SANDCASTLE. Make six new **compound words** from the following:

black	house	suit	post	master	cloth
head	card	dish	berry	case	wife

IV. Before each sentence there is a **verb.** Write the correct form of the **verb** in the space in the sentence.

1. **sing** As time passed by he —— many a song.
2. **bring** She —— fame to her town last year.
3. **kneel** They —— in prayer yesterday at the service.
4. **run** He —— a good race and came first.

V. From the verb **to pity** the adjective **pitiful** can be made. Change the **verb** before each sentence into an **adjective** and use it to fill the space in that sentence:

1. **to value** He lost a —— cargo.
2. **to thrive** He built up a —— business.
3. **to attract** She had an —— personality.
4. **to satisfy** Unless you give me a —— reason, I shall sue you.

TEST 15

I. Read very carefully through the following verses, and then answer the questions.

The Seed Shop

Here in a quiet and dusty room they lie,
Faded as crumbled stone or shifting sand,
Forlorn as ashes, shrivelled, scentless, dry—
Meadows and gardens running through my hand.

On this brown husk a dale of hawthorn dreams,
A cedar in this narrow cell is thrust
That will drink deeply of a century's streams,
These lilies shall make summer on my dust.

Here in their safe and simple house of death,
Sealed in their shells a million roses leap
Here I can blow a garden with my breath,
And in my hand a forest lies asleep.

Muriel Stuart

1. What phrase does the speaker use to describe the room where the seeds are stored?
2. Certain words and phrases help us to picture the seeds—**forlorn as ashes,** etc. From this list choose words or phrases which also describe their condition: biding their time, slumbering, sweet-smelling, fresh, carrying on their work, indestructible, looking to the future, stored temporarily, dead and gone.
3. What is the speaker doing each time seeds are named?
4. What is meant by a **dale of hawthorns?**
5. When the cedar is planted, how long might it last?
6. What does the speaker mean when she says she can **blow a garden?**
7. Why is the room **safe and simple** for the seeds?
8. **Make summer on my dust.** In a few words, what does this mean?
9. In what mood was the writer when this poem was composed? jubilant, reflective, sad, vivacious, exultant.

ANSWERS

TEST 1

I.
1. It was 'creeping round' the door-curtain.
2. Dawn; early morning.
3. Chris climbed out of the shelter. He trailed round to the kitchen door.
4. To see how much damage had been done by the air raid during the night.
5. It was slow. He trailed: meandered; wandered.
6. The smell of frying bread made it so because it meant that the normal routine of his life was continuing. His mother had lit the paraffin heater.
7. The extra bottles showed that milk had not been delivered to some regular customers because they had been bombed out or killed during the night.
8. The insurance policies were valuable. The brandy was in case of emergency.
9. Two panes of glass were broken and repaired with pieces of cardboard.
10. The air-raid shelter door had a curtain across it.
11. It meant that the air-raid was over and it was safe for everyone to return to his home; a wailing siren sounded.
12. (*b*) The Hazards of War.

II. 1. strength; 2. sympathy; 3. victor; 4. giant

III. 1. attentively; 2. stealthily; 3. soundly; 4. bitterly; 5. distinctly

IV. 1. sculptor; 2. architect; 3. explorer; 4. auctioneer

V. disadvantage, disconnect; immortal, impractical; unselfish, unimportant; invisible, incorrect

TEST 2

I.
1. For eighty-four days.
2. They were very large fish (marlin), which were to be found in those waters.
3. 'Definitely and finally salao'.
4. The old man was not catching any fish.
5. He went down to the quay to help him stow away his gear.
6. It was patched with flour sacks.
7. 'Thin and gaunt with deep wrinkles on the back of his neck.'

8. It looked like a flag of permanent defeat; gaunt.
9. His luck had run out. He was finished.
10. (b) unfortunate; (e) ill-starred; (f) disastrous

II. 1. (a) some North American Red Indians; (b) cowboys; (c) a prospector, trapper or lumberjack, or an explorer, or a family seeking a new life (in America); (d) a prisoner or a monk
2. (a) The Kings and Queens of Great Britain, at certain times; (b) The President of the United States; (c) The Prime Minister of Great Britain; (d) The Chancellor of the Exchequer

III. goal, sprinted, crossed, defenders, surprise, skywards, nodded, back, even, hundreds, scarves, waved, echoed, ground

IV. 1. poacher; 2. ancient; 3. New York; 4. cabin

V. 1. earlier; 2. most gracious; 3. most; 4. furthest

TEST 3

I. 1. On the steps of the Capitol, in Rome.
2. They were only pretending to be his friends.
3. Brutus, Cassius, Casca; Marc Antony.
4. Some were jealous of his success. Others feared he might become King.
5. Their daggers.
6. They were easily hidden. Gunpowder had not been invented.
7. The story says that the plotters thought Caesar might accept the crown of Rome.
8. (a) assassinated; (b) senators; (c) jealous; (d) had failed to do; (e) was short lived; (f) mob; (g) again and again
9. (c) With friends like these, who needs enemies?

II. 1. Where are you? We're at Uncle Arthur's looking after the girls' coats.
2. The children's dog slept in their aunt's (or aunts') house.
3. The lady's painting was taller than the man's.
4. The ladies' sculptures were smaller than the men's.
5. The boys' bicycle was faster than the girls'.
6. England's goal was due to the team's efforts.

III. 1. "What is the first lesson of the day?" asked Jim.
2. "I am not guilty," the accused man cried out.
3. "Tommy, will you be playing in the next game?" the captain asked.
4. "I have to be home early this evening!" shouted Emma suddenly.

IV. 1. cons; 2. nay; 3. punishment; 4. omega; 5. mortar;
    6. hawing
V. 1. knife; 2. knight; 3. knapsack; 4. knuckles; 5. knoll;
    6. knell

TEST 4
I. 1. (*b*) timber (logs)
   2. To make it look like a forest glade; for decoration.
   3. Resinous pine-boughs. They burned very easily.
   4. flickering
   5. Shipmen and villagers. The villagers were hosts to the shipmen.
   6. In the middle of the hall. A hole in the roof.
   7. (*b*) the hall was filled with smoke.
   8. It was blowing the smoke from the fire back into the feast hall.
   9. Many were laughing and were busy talking of their forthcoming voyage in the new ship.
   10. (*c*) A great voyage was soon to begin.
   11. feast-hall, shipmen, corn-wine, mead, platters, chimney-hole.

II. Sammy Smith would drink and eat
   From morning until night,
   He filled his mouth so full of meat,
   It was a horrid sight.
   Indeed he ate and drank so fast,
   And used to stuff and cram,
   The name they called him by at last
   Was Greedy, Greedy Sam.

III. 1. BRICK, TRICK, TRICE, TRACE, TRADE
   2. CLOWN, CROWN, BROWN, BRAWN, BRAIN

IV. 1. The band is playing a tune which I like very much.
   The tune which the band is playing I like very much etc.
   2. I am able to do what you are able to do.
   3. I have with me a witness on whose word you can rely.
   4. The player who scored the winning goal seemed inspired.

V. 1. laughable; 2. edible; 3. reachable; 4. legible

TEST 5
I. 1. (*b*) They told the soldiers that fighting was over for the night
   2. fatigue
   3. To scare away wolves. To keep them warm.

    4. His homeland.
    5. They seemed to look down and keep watch, as sentinels do.
    6. The phrase "the home of my fathers."
    7. (c) he had had enough of war
    8. (a) the night cloud had lowered; (b) overpowered; (c) thousands; (d) pallet of straw; (e) faggot; (f) the dead of the night
    9. A war of a few centuries ago, in a foreign land.
II. 1. star; 2. colourful; 3. friction; 4. peaceful
III. London, Piccadilly Circus, Knightsbridge, Oxford Circus, Marble Arch, London Transport, Underground, The Tower, St Paul's, Westminster Abbey, Hyde Park
IV. 1. fish; 2. road signs; 3. metal; 4. places of worship
V. 1. Brazil 2. Norway 3. Poland 4. Sweden 5. Greece 6. Canada

TEST 6

I. 1. He thought his uncle was playing a joke on him.
    2. In the middle of the night.
    3. Big, branching, with a thick trunk.
    4. It stood near to the house.
    5. The phrase 'it used to stand there'
    6. foreign fruits: coconuts, betel-nuts.
    7. The sky was covered with clouds.
    8. an odd time; not a person who plays jokes, a gloomy man
    9. A hurricane was approaching and the tree offered the safest refuge.
    10. (a) Get a move on!; (c) Start shinning up!; (f) Don't ask why!
    11. (a) matter-of-fact; (b) unimaginative; (c) practical
II. 1. branch; 2. voluntary; 3. prompt; 4. well-defined
III. 1. an order, an essay, an hour's time
    2. a daily paper, an evening paper, a weekly
    3. an unpaid job, a wage
    4. an offensive remark, an ambassador
IV. 1. no robbery; 2. fair lady; 3. none; 4. the sun shines
V. 1. hamlet, village, town, city, metropolis
    2. solo, duo, trio, quartette, quintette
    3. semiquaver, quaver, crotchet, minim, semibreve
    4. borough, town, county, country, continent

TEST 7

I.
1. (c) in a prison cell
2. (c) to make his escape
3. The clamps of the bed.
4. He did not have a screwdriver.
5. By breaking his jug and using some of the pieces.
6. These accidents were fairly common in the jail.
7. (c) he did not care to trouble himself
8. fragments, pieces
9. (a) he had too often assured himself; (b) Dantes had but one resource; (c) to excite suspicion; (d) departed

II. 1. prongs; 2. three; 3. wheels; 4. keel

III.
1. The orchestra filed on to the stage.
2. The visiting fifteen was captained by an Argentinian.
3. With a shout of triumph Jim bounded from his cell.
4. That song has been Top of the Pops for ages.
(2 and 4 can be questions)

IV. 1. margin; 2. marigold; 3. marsupial; 4. Martian; 5. martyr

V. 1. punch; 2. stone; 3. common; 4. grate

TEST 8

I.
1. In the main hall of the House of Ocelot.
2. A council of war.
3. Asamodo, Commander of the Royal Guard.
4. He was "a veteran" of many battles, with scars to show for it.
5. They stood at the back of the hall.
6. The phrase 'in the name of the King.'
7. There was a shout of acclamation.
8. (a) senior officers; (b) veteran, senior; (c) tense, expectant silence; (d) proclaimed; (e) to take up arms; (f) rose to their feet; (g) shout of acclamation; (h) with all the force of his lungs
9. (a) disagreed; (b) unanimously

II. 1. wholly; 2. lightning; 3. stationary; 4. right

III. mother, smother; choir, higher; guilt, quilt; muff, rough; quay, flea; pretty, witty; alarms, calms; cow, plough

IV. 1. impetuous; 2. complete; 3. supreme; 4. concord; 5. extend; 6. uniformity

V. state, things, fate, kings, down, made, spade

TEST 9

I.
1. Jo, Meg, Beth, Amy.
2. They stopped work and sang.
3. Beth.
4. (c) The ivory from which they were made had grown yellow with age.
5. A flute.
6. 'Twinkle, twinkle, little star'.
7. She played the piano whilst the others sang.
8. (a) chirped; (b) at her own sweet will; (c) a household custom; (d) lullaby
9. (b) If music be the food of love, play on.
10. Musical notes with certain time values.
11. loving, harmonious, musical, tender

II. blare (trumpet), crack (rifle), crash or bang (explosion), zoomed or buzzed (aeroplane), rattled or tinkled (teacups), drone (voice) banged (door), hoot or toot (horn)

III.
1. guilty secret, unseen danger, pleasant surprise, practical joke, careful preparation, harmonious voices
2. old world courtesy, false modesty, unfinished business, passing fancy, unanswered correspondence

IV. (a) At the telephone exchange, or whilst phoning; (b) At Cape Canaveral or a launching base for rockets; (c) whilst passing through Customs at an airport; (d) a distress signal from an aircraft or ship; (e) at a tennis match, spoken by the umpire.

V.
1. (a) await patiently a suitable time
2. (b) dismiss someone quickly and firmly
3. (c) to deal with something boldly and speedily

TEST 10

I.
1. On the quay-side, where ships tied up.
2. (b) by waving his hand
3. It was brilliantly coloured.
4. Messmates aboard ship take meals together. He would have to have joined the ship's company.
5. One who is reckless or happy-go-lucky and pays no attention to authority.
6. landsman; lubber. The two words are sometimes combined as 'land-lubber'.
7. Join the crew by signing the necessary papers. A lugger was a type of sailing vessel.

8. 'Go for a voyage.'
9. bragging, blowing his own trumpet, saucy, spruce, handsome, bewhiskered

II. 1. continue to feud; 2. cudgel; 3. Braille; 4. theodolite; 5. promontory; 6. angle

III. 1. deciduous; 2. ice-rink; 3. nor; 4. Yugoslavia; 5. music

IV. 1. lizard; 2. zebra; 3. puzzle; 4. marzipan; 5. zenith; 6. muzzle

V. Algebra, Art, Chemistry, Citizenship, English, Geography, Handwork, History, Physical Education, Physics, Religious Instruction, Zoology

TEST 11

I. 1. It was the "last splash of light" before Stradhoughton petered out and the moors "took over".
2. The sign was made from neon lighting. This is a kind of very bright strip light used in illuminated advertisements. The sign spluttered because the tubes were faulty.
3. (c) the people were stand-offish and unneighbourly
4. (b) to find a girl
5. Combing their hair and larking about to draw the attention of the girls passing by.
6. They were showing themselves off while they were waiting for their boyfriends to arrive.
7. The advert was printed on the paper bags.
8. A girl called Rita.
9. (a) promenaded; (b) escorts; (c) an amenity; (d) warily
10. high-spirited, sleazy, unkempt, rowdy, quarrelsome

II. 1. Winnie the Pooh/Christopher Robin
2. Romeo/Juliet
3. Tweedledum/Tweedledee
4. Robinson Crusoe/Man Friday
5. Antony/Cleopatra
6. Robin Hood/Maid Marian
7. Peter Pan/Wendy
8. Dr Jekyll/Mr Hyde

III. The order is 3, 1, 5, 2, 4.

IV. 1. The postmistress never saw her niece's granddaughter.
2. The Girl Guides gave a duck to the schoolgirls to keep as a pet.

3. The Duchess of Ruritania may never be a queen but her aunt might.
4. The natives thought the giantess was a goddess.

V. 1. "Oh, to be in England now that April's there," said the poet.
2. Hampstead Heath is well worth visiting on a Bank Holiday.
3. "We are about to start," said the guard. "Take your seats, please."
4. "You are going the wrong way," she snapped. "This is the road to Dorking."

TEST 12

I. 1. June 1953.
2. In Nepal, Northern India.
3. Its summit is the highest point above sea level.
4. "I challenge you to climb me."
5. Avalanches, blizzards, extreme cold, hunger.
6. Edmund Hillary and John Hunt.
7. Hillary and Tensing Norgay.
8. (a) mortals; (b) devoted; (c) reigned supreme; (d) "I challenge you!"
9. She created them Sir John Hunt and Sir Edmund Hillary.
10. Courageous, valiant, brave, indomitable.
11. Example: EVEREST CONQUERED!

II. 1. I didn't do so badly after all.
2. You are as much to blame as he is.
3. He chose the largest of the three cakes.
4. Look after your pets, as I do.

III. 1. neighbourhood; 2. centenarian; 3. immediately;
4. optimistic and pessimistic; 5. cartography

IV. 1. infertile; fictional/imagined/imaginary; 3. dissatisfied;
4. spendthrift

V. 1. spectacles, gymnasium, magazine, satisfactorily
2. 10 o'clock in the evening, Promenade, Fifth Symphony
3. Trades Union Congress, Amalgamated Engineering Union, Transport and General Workers Union
4. Royal Society for the Prevention of Cruelty to Animals, National Society for the Prevention of Cruelty to Children, United Nations Educational, Scientific and Cultural Organisation

TEST 13

I.
1. Into three parts. The terrace and the gravelled path.
2. It led to the river bank.
3. It was not well tended and cultivated.
4. Old, twisted, covered with lichen moss.
5. When touched it almost fell into their hands.
6. (*c*) plants called box-trees
7. The trees were well spread out in lines and were much taller than the children.
8. (*c*) The sun could not reach that area of grass to evaporate the dew.
9. sweet, juicy, luscious.
10. High walls.
11. A powdery deposit on the skin of the fruit which is also often found on grapes and plums.

II. 1. galaxy; 2. anthology; 3. canteen; 4. ream

III.
1. The brooches were in the women's studios.
2. The gypsies were prophets to their tribes.
3. The Members of Parliament sat in the libraries.
4. Our sisters-in-law liked the scarves.
5. Spoonfuls of those jellies for us, please.

IV. 1. emigrate; 2. satisfy; 3. imagines; 4. obey

V. 1. philatelists 2. numismatists 3. campanologists
4. palmists 5. astrologists 6. manicurists

TEST 14

I.
1. To find the buried treasure.
2. He was tied to Long John Silver.
3. Shovels, picks, food and drink.
4. At mid-day.
5. The 'tall tree' marked on the map
6. North of north-north-east.
7. They heard the shouts of one of the men who had gone on ahead.
8. (*b*) He was not afraid to go near the skeleton.
9. (*a*) armed to the teeth; (*b*) a strange crowd
10. People had used it as a look-out spot.
11. He had one leg. He sometimes had a parrot on his shoulder.

II. 1. two peas; 2 a lord; 3. houses; 4. the hills;
5. a feather

III. blackberry; headmaster; dishcloth; suitcase; housewife; postcard
IV. 1. sang; 2. brought; 3. knelt; 4. ran
V. 1. valuable; 2. thriving; 3. attractive; 4. satisfactory

TEST 15
I. 1. Quiet and dusty.
   2. biding their time, slumbering, indestructible, carrying on their work, looking to the future, stored temporarily
   3. handling them
   4. A small wood of hawthorn bushes in a valley.
   5. Sometimes for centuries. (The best cedars do not produce cones until they are forty years old).
   6. She could blow on to the different seeds and scatter them.
   7. The room was used for storing the seeds, it was dry and was not usually disturbed.
   8. Will bloom after I am dead. Will outlive me.
   9. reflective, sad

II. 1. destruction; 2. awakening; 3. ruination; 4 speech;
    5. punishment

III. 1. We/They got up at dawn, ate apples and then went into our/their private rooms.
     2. The managers knew them better than they knew themselves.
     3. Our step-daughters were maids-of-honour to queens.
     4. Flights of swallows and schools of porpoises accompanied the men-of-war.

IV. 1. The King from "The King's Breakfast"
    2. The White Rabbit
    3. The Three Musketeers, Athos, Porthos, Aramis
    4. Tom Sawyer
    5. Scheherazade
    6. Mr Willy Wonka

V.
Switzerland	Swiss	French, German, Italian according to divisions or cantons
Wales	Welsh	Welsh/English
Poland	Poles	Polish
Denmark	Danes	Danish
Spain	Spaniards	Spanish

TEST 16

I. 1. (c) a warning that suddenly appeared on the screen
    2. (c) It made him unable to believe what was happening.
    3. Tony Verdersaki.
    4. Yasko. Japanese.
    5. (b) They were going off in another direction.
    6. Three years.
    7. "We're changing course!"
    8. 0.01°, 0.02°, 0.03°, 0.04° ...
    9. Command Centre personnel; digits; stirred himself into action; urgently; horizon

II. 1. choral; 2. metallic; 3. melodious; 4. shadowy

III. 1. above; 2. against; 3. After; 4. about

IV. 1. They understood quite well his point of view.
    2. He strode into the arena, sword in hand, and laughed aloud.
    3. All the children taught one another.
    4. He forsook his comrades and fled.

V. 1. linen; 2. bassoon; 3. leopard; 4. teacher

TEST 17

I. 1. By the language—"thou comest" etc; by the story itself, which is religious history, found in the Old Testament in the Bible.
    2. David was the hero and Goliath was his enemy.
    3. A staff, a sling, five stones.
    4. The Philistine nation.
    5. A shepherd's purse.
    6. His youth, and that he had no real warlike weapons or armour.
    7. That he would give his flesh to the birds and beasts.
    8. He used one stone.
    9. Because he slew him with his sword.
    10. staff, drew nearer, disdained, took thence, smote
    11. David—little, youthful, resourceful, triumphant, victorious
        Goliath—massive, boastful, vanquished, over-confident, threatening, conquered

II. 1. owlet; 2. eaglet; 3. foal; 4. cygnet; 5. elver;
    6. cub; 7. piglet

III. 1. worst; 2. best; 3. most; 4. most careful,
    5. more beautiful; most beautiful

IV. 1. different from; 2. bigger; 3. nor; 4. taught; 5. his

V. 1. vegetarian; 2. omitted (ignored); 3. amphibian; 4. colonel 5. annually

TEST 18

I. 1. (*a*) It was not as he usually saw it.
2. The fire was being blown by the breeze which made it take on that particular shape.
3. The grass was sun-dried because it had not rained for months.
4. (*b*) It was the quickest way of clearing them.
5. The grass had been burnt off.
6. "... his beloved little valley"
7. It was biscuit-coloured (light brownish yellow).
8. "Everything'll burn off soon if we don't get rain. Me included."
9. spruce, perky, landscape, consuming, alleys, drifted away, parched
10. unusual, exceptional, unprecedented, fantastic

II. 1. blue, tan, white; 2. whey; 3. groom, cart, trap, rider; 4. thank you; 5. hungry, lanky; 6. seek

III. 1. quoit; 2. queen; 3. quadruped; 4. quote; 5. quarrel

IV. 1. lynx; 2. reins; 3. peddle; 4. parson told, sexton tolled

V. roads, twelve, ill-paved, repaired, followed, ploughed-up, wagons, frosts, ruts

TEST 19

I. 1. He was a merchant.
2. (*b*) They anchored the ship to the sea bottom.
3. The phrases "... journeyed many days from isle to isle" and "At last ..."
4. Beautiful and fair.
5. They lit fires, drank and made merry, and explored.
6. It was a whale.
7. The whale had been in one place for a long time. The sand had settled and trees had seeded.
8. They awakened the whale.
9. merchandise, made preparations, speedily, panic, desperately
10. Buying and selling requires money to change hands. Exchanging means giving one article for another.

II. 1. Register; 2. Catalogue; 3. Telephone Directory; 4. Dictionary; 5. Atlas; 6. Biography; Autobiography if

written by the person about his own life;   7. Ship's Log;
   8. Diary
III. 1. froze;   2. overheard;   3. bore, slept;   4. came, spun;
   5. bade
IV. 1. You shouldn't expect kindness in a thieves' kitchen.
   2. Where there's a will there's relations.
   3. The King's Secretary's bag was lost.
   4. The oak trees' boughs were stout, but the fir tree's boughs were slim.
   5. The babies' prams were new but one baby's bottle was empty.
V. 1. "Stand and deliver!" roared the highwayman.
   2. "The Prime Minister has come home with good news," the broadcaster announced.
   3. The man asked, "Will you dance the polka with me?"
   4. "Come into the garden, Maud," sang the poet.

TEST 20

I. 1. He had known no change.
   2. He was gathering shells.
   3. (*b*) great surprise
   4. They were sailing-ships. He had never seen any type of boat other than a canoe.
   5. The wind in the sails.
   6. The sails and the flags and bunting.
   7. Small, light, fast sailing ships; Columbus.
   8. That this was the end of the simple life and that 'civilisation' was coming.
   9. (*c*) It was the custom of the country.
   10. strayed, a strange commingled noise, bellying, slant
II. 1. WIFE, WIRE, HIRE, HARE, HARP
   2. POLO, POLE, PALE, GALE, GAME
III. 1. (*c*) scold or punish;   2. (*a*) lead the way;
   3. (*b*) escape by running
IV. Alice in Wonderland, Charlie and the Chocolate Factory, King Solomon's Mines, Little Women, National Velvet, Railway Children (The), Robinson Crusoe, Tom Sawyer, Watership Down, What Katy Did
V. 1. chicks;   2. trains;   3. wood;   4. fables

TEST 21

I.
1. (e) They were against the rules.
2. They were in the furze hill behind the college. They were made by hollowing out the bushes.
3. Stalky, Beetle and M'Turk.
4. They smoked.
5. Both masters kept a careful watch on the boys' activities.
6. A hawk hovers silently in the air, watching, then swiftly descends upon its prey. Foxy would secretly watch the boys through his binoculars and then suddenly pounce on them.
7. (c) he had studied the boys' habits
8. lairs; meditation; subtle; Providence; pugs
9. The story was written in 1899.
10. a boarding school or college
11. He was the master responsible for physical education at the school which mostly consisted of drill or marching.

II. deeds, weeds, grow, snow, fall, wall, fly, sky

III.
1. quickly, descended
2. quietly, inaudible
3. immovable
4. retreat

IV.
1. The Marchioness acted like a comedienne.
2. The instructress complained to the headmistress.
3. The heiress to the throne had a number of peahens.
4. "Enter Mrs Jones, the baroness and the Indian squaw."

V. Order of sentences: 4, 2, 6, 1, 3, 5

TEST 22

I.
1. Polyphemus.
2. In a cave.
3. They heard the tramping of many feet and the bleating of ewes.
4. He was a huge as a mountain and he had one red eye in the middle of his forehead.
5. They fled to the darkest corner of the cave.
6. There were ewes already in the courtyard.
7. Half was drunk and half was curdled for cheese.
8. A tremendous boulder.
9. A huge log for his fire.
10. conversing, casting fearful glances, ewes, fearful monster, huge as a mountain, intruders

11. tremendous, gigantic, monstrous, fearsome, formidable, horrific

II. Kew, Ellen Gee, you, tea, why, bee, eye, see

III. 1. botanist; 2. chemist; 3. arsonist; 4. bigamist

IV. 1. prattle becomes rattle
2. clout becomes lout
3. steak becomes teak
4. trough becomes rough

V. 1. leisure; 2. hunt; 3. dexterity; 4. confident

TEST 23

I. 1. They were English.
2. Forty.
3. The "Rose". It had been destroyed by fire.
4. They were the first men to explore the area so none of the rivers was named on the charts or maps.
5. Canoe.
6. They had died in the mountains.
7. Rio Negro, Indians, Andes, jungle, poisoned arrows, tribesmen, crocodiles
8. They had no combs or razors.
9. They had repaired their torn garments with cloth or material woven by the Indians.
10. There were no tracks for them to follow and they had no maps.
11. charred, remains, untrodden hills, uncharted, survivors, sundried

II. Rugby Unions, Triple Crown, England, Wales, Scotland, Ireland, France, Grand Slam. England, Twickenham; Wales, National Stadium in Cardiff; Scotland, Murrayfield, Edinburgh; Ireland, Landsdowne Road, Dublin; France, Stade Colombes. All Blacks, New Zealand; Kiwis, Australia; Pumas, Argentina; Japanese

III. 1. sweetness; 2. eight legs; 3. summit; 4. brim

IV. 1. Clans; 2. The Great Lakes; 3. A rainbow; 4. National Emblems

V. 1. "I owe you five farthings," say the Bells of St Martin's.
2. "Come in," the Mayor cried, looking bigger.
3. The actor recited "The Knave of Hearts he stole some tarts".
4. "You'll never get away with it," said the policeman. "I'll be watching you."

TEST 24

I.
1. A small stone barn. By means of a wooden partition.
2. The senior, or older children.
3. One dame teacher.
4. The boys and girls came 'from miles around'.
5. At fourteen.
6. The History lesson.
7. Unusual fertility.
8. The working fields and the factories.
9. (b) made their daily excursions to the school
10. Dame, dreary image, one up on our poor old grandparents; at its peak, oaths, odours
11. The children brought 'curious pies' to school.

II.
1. The naughty child, or the wrong-doer who had disgraced his family.
2. A day of great importance (e.g. a birthday).
3. Written plainly and clearly.
4. Descended from royalty or from a family of great importance.

III. 1. death; 2. grass; 3. post; 4. barrel

IV.
1. Queen's Counsel, United Nations, Very Important Person, Order of Merit
2. Youth Hostel Association, Young Men's Christian Association, Order of the British Empire
3. Her Majesty's Ship, Women's Voluntary Service
4. Madame, Monsieur (Mrs Mr)

V. aught; heir; died; bier; borough

TEST 25

I.
1. By the chalk pit.
2. (b) to stop them from straying
3. The phrase 'the further dusk and dew' tells us.
4. Its light was reflected in the water.
5. 'The cricketers had done'.
6. 'The clattering wheels went past and died away'.
7. They had stolen them.
8. Mouth organs.
9. They smoked pipes.
10. Not one of them seemed to have any cares.
11. anew, the horses supped, goss, the last sunset glowed, churr, leas, lolled, gossipped, worked toys with piths of reed
12. (a) Rustic joys.

II. 1. caravan;   2. caraway;   3. carbine;   4. carbuncle;
5. carcase;   6. carton;   7. carp;   8. carnation;   9. carol;
10. carnivore

III. 1. to beg;   2. warder;   3. receipt;   4. indolent;   5. adroit

IV. Not, Celia, that I juster am,
Or better than the rest,
For I would change each hour like them,
Were not my heart at rest,
But I am tied to very thee
By every thought I have,
Thy face I only care to see,
Thy heart I only crave.

V. 1. He had no reply although he shouted many times.
2. Neither Archie nor Dennis is handsome.
3. The field was packed with people who were all applauding excitedly.
4. You have tested the car which Father wants to buy for us.

TEST 26

I. 1. In Friers Street.
2. It occupied a commanding position.
3. Golden boys and golden grapes.
4. It seemed to invite the passer-by to stop and look at himself.
5. By placing several mirrors around the flame to reflect the image.
6. Dining room.
7. (c) they did not feel middle aged at that time
8. premises; flares out extravagantly, platoons of candles, on closer inspection, to contemplate himself
9. (a) artistic, talented, imaginative
(b) well-to-do, refined, affluent, well-heeled
10. When he or she is learning a trade and has agreed to work for a period of time for a small wage in return for being taught.
11. Because he had only just arrived.

II. 1. for;   2. from;   3. off;   4. to;   5. with;   6. of

III. 1. Richard III;   2. Sir Francis Drake;
3. Collectors during the Great Plague of London 1665;
4. King Canute;   5. Sir Winston Churchill

IV. 1. think alike;   2. catches the worm;   3. before a fall;
4. and spoil the child

V. 1. books; 2. manufactured goods; 3. children or plants; 4. water, usually for drinking; 5. bees; 6. grain, in store

TEST 27

I. 1. Its boundary was the river.
2. Hedges, fences or wire netting.
3. "the softly flowing water"
4. (*b*) in case she should fall into the river and drown
5. He was older than his sister, and could swim.
6. Nothing had ever landed there and it had not been built for that purpose.
7. So that he could fill his watering-can from the river more easily.
8. (*a*) like all the others; (*b*) quite out of the ordinary; (*c*) brought to a stop
9. Because it had been built in the year of Queen Victoria's jubilee, or some similar event.

II. 1. miserable; 2. gather; 3. healthiness; 4. positive; 5. choice

III. frozen/boatswain (bosun); sou'wester/Leicester; gaol/pale; humming/coming; goal/whole; Delhi/Nelly

IV. market-gardener; chicken-hearted; sledge-hammer; engine-driver; oil-lamp; drinking-water; homesick

V. illegal, irregular, disapprove, insincere, misbehave, abnormal, ignoble, nonessential, unselfish, impolite

TEST 28

I. 1. Youthful private.
2. (*b*) in listening to the talk of other soldiers
3. Marches and attacks.
4. (*c*) He wanted to think things out.
5. He went to his hut. A bed built on a frame or into a recess often with a second bed above it.
6. Cracker (biscuit) boxes serving as furniture.
7. A folded tent.
8. (*a*) at last he was going to fight
9. with eager ears, varied comments, to be alone with some new thoughts, an intricate hole, he was obliged to labour to make himself believe, in a little trance of astonishment
10. The North V The South; The Federals V the Confederates;

The Union V the Confederacy

II. 1. mountainous; 2. meteoric; 3. atmospheric; 4. arithmetical; 5. comfortable; 6. telescopic

III. 1. Chelsea; 2. Norwich; 3. Watford; 4. Everton; 5. Preston; 6. Fulham

IV. 1. violincello, omnibus, pianoforte
2. State Registered Nurse; Superintendent; Union of Soviet Socialist Republics
3. Postscript, Professor, Doctor of Philosophy
4. Pay as you earn, General Headquarters

V. In this order: 5, 1, 2, 4, 3, 6

TEST 29

I. 1. For fifty-five years. The sixteenth century.
2. Spain.
3. They were great explorers.
4. (c) a description of her poets and playwrights
5. potatoes, tomatoes, turkeys, tobacco
6. India, Russia
7. (b) She brought England safely through trying times.
8. exploring, foreigners, for ever and ever
9. For their heroism, voyages and discoveries.
10. Example: Hamlet; Julius Caesar; A Midsummer Night's Dream—Shakespeare: Dr Faustus; Tamburlaine—Marlowe: The Faerie Queen—Spenser

II. 1. The passers-by saw the hangers-on ignore the bye-laws and break the curios.
2. The thieves took the loaves from the shelves and cut them with knives.
3. The cowboys with the lassos/lassoes rode broncos at the rodeos.
4. The cacti grew on plateaus/plateaux, but the sheep ate them.

III. 1. generous; 2. flexible; 3. exhale; 4. opaque; 5. innocent

IV. athletics, badminton, baseball, basketball, boxing, cricket, football, golf, hockey, lacrosse, rugby, squash, water-polo

V. In this order: carafe, tumbler, brief-case, thermos-flask, wardrobe, trunk, handbag, make-up, tank, petrol, zoo, animals

TEST 30

I.
1. The sounds made by the singing birds.
2. The best season of the year.
3. Sprays of flowers and leaves to decorate the house. They were bright and colourful.
4. (c) They play sweet music upon their pipes.
5. Because in the countryside people went barefoot.
6. Pleasant perfumes, the scents of the grasses and bushes.
7. (a) sting; (b) merry lay
8. Young lovers meet.
9. (b) Rural simplicity.

II. 1. Red Admiral; 2. blue stocking; 3. brown study; 4. Blue Peter; 5. Black Death

III. 1. rugby; 2. Lilliputian; 3. billiards/snooker; 4. dale; 5. Paris

IV.
1. The boy said that he was sorry.
2. The coach said that he liked the style of Jim's batting.
3. Gorging Jack told Guzzling Jimmy that he was extremely hungaree.
4. The shop assistant said that the tea-set cost £25.

V. 1. emigrate; 2. now; 3. equinox;
4. clearly/intelligibly/succinctly etc.

II. From the verb **to free** the noun **freedom** can be made. Change the **verb** before each sentence into a **noun,** and use it to fill the space in that sentence.

1. TO DESTROY   You are in danger of ——.
2. TO AWAKE   Each dawn his —— was troubled and noisy.
3. TO RUIN   Your behaviour will lead to your ——.
4. TO SPEAK   That was a marvellous —— you delivered.
5. TO PUNISH   Misbehaviour will lead to ——.

III. Rewrite these sentences in **plural** form:

1. I got up at dawn, ate an apple and then went to my private room.
2. The manager knew him better than he knew himself.
3. My step-daughter was a maid-of-honour to a queen.
4. A flight of swallows and a school of porpoises accompanied the man-of-war.

IV. Name these characters from fiction who said:

1. "I do like a little bit of butter on my bread."
2. "I'm late for a very important date."
3. "All for one and one for all!"

Who were these people?

4. He painted a fence white, with much help.
5. She told stories in the Arabian Nights for a thousand-and-one nights.
6. He owned a really unusual chocolate factory.

V. Look at this:

Country: Turkey;   **People:** Turks;   **Language:** Turkish

Now complete this list:

Country	**People**	**Language**
Switzerland		
Wales		
Poland		
Denmark		
Spain		

TEST 16

I. Read very carefully through the following passage, and then answer the questions.

Space 1999. Mind-Breaks of Space

It hit them from out of nowhere. The moment was so unexpected and sudden that even Commander John Koenig himself was stunned into inaction. He could only stand and stare in amazement with the rest of the Command Centre personnel as the warning letters flashed up on the Big Screen: CHANGE OF HORIZON. The slow certain flickers of the digits below told the progress of the alarming event: 0.01°, 0.02°, 0.03°, 0.04°...

"John," questioned Tony Verdersaki urgently. "What in God's name...? We're changing course!"

The Security Chief's words broke the spell of shock. Koenig stirred himself into action. "I see it, but I don't understand it," he said. He glanced urgently over his shoulder. "Yasko," he ordered, "show me the horizon." The Japanese operator punched a new set of directions for the computer. Abruptly, the grey blankness against which the coded computer of the last three years had been flashing—all that had been collected since the Moon had blasted free of its earth orbit—began to clear.

Michael Butterworth and J. Jeff Jones

1. What hit the crew of the space-craft **from nowhere?** (*a*) a collision with another space-ship; (*b*) a missile from the enemy; (*c*) a warning that suddenly appeared on the screen.
2. What effect did this have on the Commander? (*a*) it made him shout with joy; (*b*) it told him all was well; (*c*) it made him unable to believe what was happening.
3. What was the Security Officer's name.
4. Who was in charge of the computer? What was his nationality?
5. What did the screen foretell? (*a*) that everything was in order; (*b*) that they were going off in another direction; (*c*) that there was no need to worry unduly.
6. For how long had the space-ship been on an even course?
7. What three words spoken by the Security Officer showed that he had begun to understand what was happening?
8. What lines on the computer showed the progress of events?

9. Write down the words and phrases that mean: crew, numbers, pulled himself together, hurriedly, the point where earth and sky seemed to meet.

II. From the noun **sorrow** we can make the adjective **sorrowful.** Make an adjective from the **noun** in front of each sentence and use it to fill the space:

1. **choir**   The class formed a —— society.
2. **metal**   As the spade struck the soil there was a —— ring.
3. **melody**   What a —— tone the singer produced.
4. **shadow**   All around him were —— forms.

III. Complete the sentences below using the **correct word** from this list: **above, about, after, against.**

1. The kite soared —— the rooftops.
2. Will you fight for me or —— me?
3. —— the ball was over, the princess hurried home.
4. They are saying unkind things —— me.

IV. Change these sentences from **present tense to past tense:**

1. They understand quite well his point of view.
2. He strides into the arena, sword in hand, and laughs aloud.
3. All the children teach one another.
4. He forsakes his comrades and flees.

V. (boy, man, lad)—(girl, woman, **nephew**). Of the three words in the second bracket, the word **nephew** is nearest in meaning to the words in the first bracket, all being **male.**
Now do the same with these:

1. (woollen, silken, cotton)—(nylon, terylene, linen)
2. (oboe, flute, clarinet)—(trombone, bassoon, trumpet)
3. (jaguar, panther, tiger)—(antelope, leopard, zebra)
4. (master, instructor, tutor)—(pupil, teacher, student)

TEST 17

I. Read very carefully through the following passage, and then answer the questions.

David Slays Goliath

David took his staff in his hand and chose him five smooth stones and put them in a shepherd's purse which he had. His sling was in his hand and he drew nearer to Goliath. The Philistine came on unto David, and when he looked about him and saw David he disdained him for he was but a youth. And he said unto David, "Am I a dog that thou comest against me with stones? I will give thy flesh unto the fowls of the air and to the beasts of the field."

And David put his hand into his bag and took thence a stone and slung it and smote the Philistine on the forehead, that the stone sank into his forehead. He fell upon his face to the earth. And David ran to the Philistine, took his sword from the sheath, slew him and cut off his head. And when the Philistines saw that their champion was dead, they fled.

1. How do we know that this is a story of long ago? In what book can we read the full story?
2. Who was the hero of the story, and who was his enemy?
3. What weapons did the hero carry?
4. Of what nation was Goliath a member?
5. What word is used for a shepherd's bag?
6. Why did David's appearance make Goliath so angry?
7. What did Goliath boast that he would do to David?
8. How many stones did David use?
9. How do we know that the stone did not kill Goliath, but merely stunned him?
10. Find words and phrases that mean: stick or pole, approached, looked with scorn, from the bag, struck.
11. Divide these words into two groups, those that describe David, and those that describe Goliath: little, massive, boastful, youthful, resourceful, vanquished, triumphant, over-confident, victorious, threatening, conquered.

II. A young bear is a **cub.** Write down the names for the young of the following creatures:

1. owl
2. eagle
3. horse
4. swan
5. eel
6. leopard
7. pig

III. Jack is **small,** Sam is **smaller,** Pete is the **smallest** of the three. In the same way, fill in the spaces in the following sentences:

1. Peter's work is **bad,** Paul's work is **worse,** but Percy's is the ——.
2. Today Peter's work is **good,** Paul's work is **better,** but Percy's is the ——.
3. Peter won many **marks,** Paul won **more,** but Percy won the ——.
4. Peter's work was **careful,** Paul's work was more **careful,** but Percy's was the ——.
5. Monday was a **beautiful** day, Tuesday was ——, but Wednesday was the ——.

IV. There are errors in each of the following sentences. Rewrite these sentences correctly.

1. Your school uniform is different to mine.
2. Why is it you always have the biggest of the two apples?
3. Neither Joe or Jill would confess.
4. You have learnt him some useful things.
5. Each of the boys had their chance.

V. Write **single words** for these:

1. One who will not eat the flesh of animals.
2. Left out, or not included.
3. A creature that can live on land or in water.
4. An officer in charge of a regiment.
5. Happening once a year.

TEST 18

I. Read very carefully through the following passage, and then answer the questions.

Pop Larkins

After parking the Rolls Royce between the pigsties and the muck-heap where twenty young turkeys were lazily scratching in the hot mid-morning air, Pop Larkins, looking spruce and perky in a biscuit-coloured summer suit, paused to look back across his beloved little valley.

The landscape, though so familiar to him, presented a strange sight. Half-way up the slope, in fiercely brilliant sunlight, strawberry fields were on fire. Little cockscombs of orange flame were running before a light breeze, consuming yellow alleys of straw. Behind them the fields spread black, smoking slowly with low blue clouds that drifted away to spread across parched meadows all as yellow as the straw itself after months without rain.

"Burning the strawberry fields off," Pop tóld Ma as he went into the kitchen.

"Everything'll burn off soon if we don't get rain," Ma said. "Me included, as I said to the gentleman who was here this morning."

H. E. Bates

1. Why did the landscape seem strange to Pop Larkins? (*a*) it was not as he usually saw it; (*b*) his eyesight was poor; (*c*) he was the worse for drink.
2. A cockscomb is the reddish-yellow crest on a cockerel's head. Why did the author use the phrase **little cockscombs of flame running before a light breeze?**
3. Why were the fields yellower than usual?
4. Why were the strawberry fields burning? (*a*) an arsonist had been at work; (*b*) it was the quickest way of clearing them; (*c*) it was an accidental fire.
5. Why were the fields beyond black in colour?
6. What words tell us that Pop Larkins was very fond of his surroundings?
7. What was the colour of Pop Larkin's suit?
8. What was it that Ma said to the gentleman who had called

earlier?

9. Find words and phrases that mean: neatly dressed, saucy, devouring, narrow lanes, floated, bone-dry.
10. **The Rolls Royce between the pig-sties.** Choose words and phrases to describe this sight: commonplace, unusual, everyday, natural, exceptional, unprecedented, fantastic.

II. The word **sage** is often linked with the word **onions.** Write down the words that often go with those printed below. There may be more than one answer to some of them.

1. Black and ——
2. Curds and ——
3. Horse and ——
4. Please and ——
5. Lean and ——
6. Hide and ——

III. The following words begin with **Q**. Write them down.

1. Q---T   A flattish ring for throwing at a mark.
2. Q---N   Monarch.
3. Q-------D   Four-footed animal.
4. Q---E   Recite or repeat exactly.
5. Q-----L   Argue violently.

IV. Some words have a **similar sound** but are **spelt** differently. Choose the correct word from the brackets:

1. The (links, lynx) escaped from the zoo.
2. Hold the (reins, rains) tightly Janet!
3. Go (peddle, pedal) your wares in the next street.
4. The parson (tolled, told) the sexton and the sexton (tolled, told) the bell.

V. Rewrite the paragraph below using words from the list to fill each of the spaces: twelve, ruts, ill-paved, ploughed-up, roads, repaired, wagons, followed, frosts.

The —— even within —— miles of London were at that time ——, seldom —— and very badly made up. The path the riders —— had been —— by the wheels of heavy —— and rendered rotten by the —— and thaws of the winter. Deep holes and —— were worn into the soil.

TEST 19

I. Read very carefully through the following passage, and then answer the questions.

The First Voyage of Sinbad the Sailor

I bought a large quantity of merchandise and made preparations for a long voyage. Then, with a company of traders, I set sail from Baghdad and journeyed many days from isle to isle, buying, selling and exchanging wherever we dropped anchor. At last we came to a little island that seemed very beautiful.

The passengers went ashore, lit fires, and were soon busy cooking and washing. Some began to eat, drink and be merry, whilst others set out to explore the fair isle. Suddenly the captain cried aloud from the ship, "Come aboard speedily. Leave everything and run for your lives. God be with you, for this is no island, but a huge whale floating on the surface of the ocean. On its back sands have settled and trees have grown. The heat from your fires has awakened it. It will plunge below the surface and all will be lost."

Immediately, there was panic. Terrified visitors threw themselves into the sea. Those who could, swam desperately towards the ship.

1. What occupation or trade did Sinbad follow?
2. **We dropped anchor.** Does this mean: (*a*) the sailors played a game called Crown and Anchor; (*b*) they anchored the ship to the sea bottom; (*c*) they carelessly allowed the anchor to fall overboard.
3. How do we know that it was some time before they came to the little island?
4. What two words in the story tell us that the island was pretty?
5. What did the passengers do when they went ashore?
6. In reality, what was the island?
7. How had the island become sandy and covered with trees?
8. What effect did the fires have on the island?
9. Find words or phrases that mean: goods, made plans, as quickly as you can, loss of control, hopelessly.
10. What is the difference between **buying** and **selling,** and **exchanging?**

II. Here are some questions about different kinds of books. In which book would you look to find:

1. Attendance at a school or college.
2. A list of goods or books.
3. A person's telephone number.
4. The meaning of a certain word.
5. The position of a town on a map.
6. Someone's life story (two answers)
7. The daily happenings on board a ship.
8. What happened to a person each day.

III. Change these sentences from the **present** to the **past** tense:

1. The water **freezes** in the extreme cold.
2. The master **overhears** the gossip.
3. He **bears** his heavy burden and **sleeps** soundly.
4. The spiders **come** early and **spin** their webs.
5. He **bids** me be of good courage.

IV. Write out these sentences putting the **apostrophe** into its correct place:

1. You shouldnt expect kindness in a thieves kitchen.
2. Where theres a will theres relations.
3. The Kings Secretarys bag was lost.
4. The oak trees (plural) boughs were stout, but the fir trees (singular) boughs were slim.
5. The babies prams were new but one babys bottle was empty.

V. Put the necessary **punctuation marks, capital letters** etc. into these sentences:

1. stand and deliver roared the highwayman.
2. the prime minister has come home with good news the broadcaster announced.
3. the man asked will you dance the polka with me.
4. come into the garden maud sang the poet

TEST 20

I. Read very carefully through the following verses, and then answer the questions.

There Was An Indian

There was an Indian who had known no change,
Who strayed content along a sunlit beach
Gathering shells. He heard a sudden strange
Commingled noise; looked up and gasped for speech.

For in the bay, where nothing was before,
Moved on the sea, by magic, huge canoes,
With bellying cloths on poles, and not one oar,
And fluttering coloured signs, and clambering crews.

And he, in fear, this naked man alone,
His fallen hands forgetting all their shells,
His lips gone pale, knelt low behind a stone,
And stared, and saw, and did not understand,
Columbus' doom-burdened caravels
Slant to the shore, and all their seamen land.

J. C. Squire

1. How are we told that the Indian's life had gone on day after day in the same way?
2. What was the Indian doing at the time?
3. What made him gasp for speech? (*a*) tiredness; (*b*) great surprise; (*c*) a sudden illness.
4. What really were the **huge canoes?** Why did the Indian think of them as canoes?
5. He thought they were moved **by magic.** What was the magic?
6. What were the **cloths on the poles,** and **coloured signs?**
7. What were **caravels** and who was the captain of the voyage?
8. What was the **doom** with which the ships were laden?
9. Why was the man naked? (*a*) because someone had stolen his clothes; (*b*) because he had outgrown them; (*c*) because that was the custom of the country.
10. Find words or phrases in the story which mean: wandered, a mixture of noises, swelling, move at an angle.

II. Beginning with the word MOON, and changing only one letter at a time, we can make the word BOAT, in this way: MOON, MOAN, MOAT, BOAT. We call this a **word ladder.** Now do these:

1.   WIFE   2.   POLO
Metal drawn out into   Long, slender piece of
thread   - - - -   wood   - - - -
To pay for the use of   - - - -   Of whiteish complexion   - - - -
Small, speedy animal   - - - -   High wind   - - - -
                                HARP   GAME

III. Here are some **everyday expressions.** Choose the **phrase** that means nearly the same as the expression.

Example: 'To look on the bright side' means 'to keep smiling.'

1. **'Haul over the coals'** means (*a*) bring the coal from the cellar; (*b*) convey the coal from the pit; (*c*) scold or punish.
2. **'Blaze the trail'** means (*a*) to lead the way; (*b*) wear one's blazer; (*c*) set fire to the woodland path.
3. **'Show a clean pair of heels'** means (*a*) to have neat and shiny shoes; (*b*) escape by running; (*c*) wash one's feet carefully.

IV. Write these books in **alphabetical order** as in a book catalogue:

King Solomon's Mines, What Katy Did, Alice in Wonderland, Charlie and the Chocolate Factory, Robinson Crusoe, The Railway Children, Watership Down, National Velvet, Little Women, Tom Sawyer.

V. Complete the following sentences.

Example: **Man** is to **woman** as **boy** is to ——. The missing word is **girl.**

1. **Nursery** is to **plants** as **incubator** is to ——.
2. **Heathrow** is to **aeroplanes** as **Paddington** is to ——.
3. **Lawnmower** is to **grass** as **sandpaper** is to ——.
4. **Grimm** is to **fairy-tales** as **Aesop** is to ——.

TEST 21

I. Read very carefully through the following passage, and then answer the questions.

Finding a Lodge

In summer all right-minded boys built huts in the furze-hill behind the College—little lairs whittled out of the heart of the prickly bushes, full of stumps, odd root ends and spikes, but since they were strictly forbidden, palaces of delight. And for the fifth summer in succession, Stalky, M'Turk and Beetle (this was before they reached the dignity of a study) had built, like beavers, a place of retreat and meditation, where they smoked.

Now there was nothing in their characters, as known to Mr Prout, their house-master, at all commanding respect; nor did Foxy, the subtle, red-haired school Sergeant, trust them. His business was to wear tennis shoes, carry binoculars, and swoop hawk-like upon evil boys. Had he taken the field alone, that hut would have been raided, for Foxy knew the manners of his quarry; but Providence moved Mr Prout, whose school name derived from the size of his feet, was Hoofer, to investigate on his own account; and it was the cautious Stalky who found the track of his pugs.

Rudyard Kipling

1. Why were the huts especially delightful to the boys? (*a*) because there was music laid on; (*b*) because they were comfortable; (*c*) because they were against the rules.
2. Where were the hidden places and how were they made?
3. Who occupied the hut named in the story?
4. What did they do in the lair that was expressly forbidden?
5. How do we know that Mr Prout and Foxy did not trust them?
6. Foxy would swoop **hawk-like.** Explain this.
7. Why did Foxy have a better chance of surprising his prey than did Mr Prout? (*a*) he had the gift of invisibility; (*b*) he wore various disguises; (*c*) he had studied the boys' habits.
8. What words or phrases mean: dens, quiet thinking, crafty, good luck, footprints.
9. When do you think this story was written?
10. What sort of school did the boys attend?

11. Why do you think the school had a sergeant and what would his duties have been?

II. Choose the most suitable **rhyming word** to finish each line of poetry:

A man of words and not of (**performance, deeds, doing**)
Is like a garden full of (**seeds, clay, weeds**)
And when the weeds begin to (**sprout, grow, fade**)
He's like a garden full of (**snow, rain, show**)
And when the snow begins to (**melt, fall, run**)
He's like a bird upon the (**gate, hedge, wall**)
And when the bird away does (**race, fly, shoot**)
He's like an eagle in the (**sky, heavens, sun**)

III. Write down the words **opposite** in meaning to those in heavy type:

Example: the boy **laughed** at the news.   (**cried**).

1. Walking **slowly** we **ascended** the hill.
2. If you speak **loudly** you are **audible**.
3. Are you sure that piano is **movable**?
4. The general's order caused the armies to **advance**.

IV. Change all the **masculine** words into **feminine**:

Example: **He** is my **brother**. **She** is my **sister**.

1. The marquis acted like a comedian.
2. The instructor complained to the headmaster.
3. The heir to the throne had a number of peacocks.
4. "Enter Mr Jones, the baron and the Indian brave."

V. Rearrange these sentences into the correct order.

1. He thought it was another dog.
2. He carried it away to the country.
3. He opened his mouth to snarl.
4. One day a dog stole a bone.
5. The bone fell into the stream.
6. As he was crossing over a bridge he saw his reflection in the water.

TEST 22

I. Read very carefully through the following passage, and then answer the questions.

Odysseus and Polyphemus

Whilst they sat conversing in low tones, casting fearful glances towards the cavern's mouth, all at once they heard the tramping of many feet, accompanied by loud bleatings which were answered by the ewes in the courtyard. In came Polyphemus driving his flocks before him. At the sight of that fearful monster, huge as a mountain, with one vast red eye glaring in the middle of his forehead, Odysseus and his comrades fled to the darkest corner of the cave.

The Cyclops bore in one hand a mighty log for his evening fire. Flinging it down with a crack that awakened echoes within the cavern, he closed the entrance with an immense boulder, which served as a door. He sat down to milk his ewes. Half of the milk he curdled for cheese, half he kept for drinking.

The fire blazed up. He caught sight of the intruders and cried out "Who are ye that dare come into the cave of Polyphemus?"

1. Cyclops was the name of the monster's tribe. What was the name of the Cyclops in this story?
2. Were Odysseus and his companions in a hut, a castle, a cave or a prison?
3. How did they know that danger was approaching?
4. Why was Polyphemus's appearance so horrifying?
5. Where did the men try to hide?
6. He drove his flock into the cave. How do we know that part of the flock was already waiting outside?
7. What became of the milk that Polyphemus obtained?
8. What formed the door of Polyphemus's den?
9. What did Polyphemus carry in his hand?
10. Find words or phrases that mean: talking together, looking anxiously around, female sheep, ogre, enormous, people who enter where they have no right to go.
11. Choose words from this list which describe Polyphemus: tremendous, gigantic, undersized, dwarfish, monstrous, fearsome, attractive, formidable, horrific, delightful.

II. In the following verses, **capital letters** have been substituted for words. Write down the words for which they stand.

> **Miss Ellen Gee of Kew**
> Peerless yet hopeless maid of Q
> Accomplished LNG
> Never again shall I see U,
> Together sip our T,
> For oh! the fates I know not Y,
> Sent midst the flowers a B,
> Which, venomous, stung her in the I,
> So that she could not C.

III. There is one word to describe each of the following people. All the words end in IST.

1. One who studies the natural history of plants.
2. One who deals in medical drugs.
3. One who sets fire to buildings.
4. One who marries more than once, illegally.

IV. If we chop the first letter off a fruit—**Pear,** we get 'that with which we hear'—**ear** (**Pear** becomes **ear**). Do the same with these:

1. 'To talk rather childishly' becomes 'a baby's toy'.
2. 'A harsh blow' becomes 'an awkward fellow'.
3. 'A piece of meat' becomes 'a type of wood'.
4. 'Where animals feed' becomes 'uneven or irregular'.

V. (**boy, man, lad**)—(girl, woman, **nephew**). Of the three words in the second bracket, the word **nephew** is nearest in meaning to the three words in the first as they are all male words. Now do these:

1. (repose, rest, relaxation)—(disturbance, toil, leisure)
2. (pursuit, chase, shadow)—(avoid, hunt, flee)
3. (skill, cleverness, ability)—(dexterity, incompetence, awkwardness)
4. (certain, sure, positive)—(doubtful, confident, mistrustful)

TEST 23

I. Read very carefully through the following passage, and then answer the questions.

Deep in the Jungle

Three years had passed since the band of Englishmen left their camp above the charred remains of the "Rose" and marched onwards into the jungle. Through untrodden hills, down uncharted streams they wandered. Now, forty-four of the eighty-four who started were resting on the banks of an unknown river. Their canoes were drawn up near them.

Where were the rest? Drew and five brave fellows lay at the Rio Negro, slain by the poisoned arrows of Indians; two more slept amid the valleys of the Andes, frozen to death; four more were drowned in the rapids; five or six were left behind with friendly tribesmen. Fever, snakes, crocodiles had taken the others.

The survivors were sun-dried and lean, but strong and bold as ever. Their beards were grown long, their hair was knotted, their clothes patched with native materials. Many wore the skins of animals. Their bullets were gone long since, but their swords were bright and sharp as of old.

Charles Kingsley

1. What was the nationality of the men who took part in the expedition?
2. Of the original party, how many were no longer present?
3. What was the name of the ship? What had happened to it?
4. Why didn't they know the name of the river?
5. What had been their means of transport?
6. **Slept amid the valleys of the Andes.** What does this mean?
7. Which three proper nouns and which other nouns tell us that this took place in a foreign land.
8. Why were their beards long and their hair matted?
9. Explain the phrase: **patched with native materials?**
10. They **wandered.** Why is this word used?
11. Find words and phrases that mean: burnt, all that was left, where no one had before set foot, not shown on maps, those who had come through the dangers, tanned.

II. Rewrite this paragraph using a **capital letter** at the beginning of each **proper noun:**

Four rugby unions compete each for the triple crown, england wales, scotland and ireland. france joins them for the grand slam. england plays at twickenham, wales at the national stadium in cardiff, scotland at murrayfield, edinburgh, and ireland at landsdown road, dublin. france plays at stade colombes. the all blacks of new zealand and the kiwis of australia are welcome visitors. the pumas of argentina and the japanese also pay visits.

III. Think of the word **water.** It need not be **stagnant,** or **coloured,** but it is always **wet.** Choose one word from the brackets that is always related to the word before the bracket:

1. **sugar** (whiteness, sweetness, crystals)
2. **spider** (web, prey, eight legs)
3. **mountain** (snowcap, forest, summit)
4. **sombrero** (decorative, brim, leather)

IV. Look at each group below. What words would you use to **group** each one:

1. MacDonald, Campbell, Grant, MacPherson, Stewart.
2. Huron, Ontario, Michigan, Erie, Superior.
3. Red, orange, yellow, green, blue, indigo, violet.
4. Thistle, shamrock, rose, daffodil, fleur-de-lys.

V. Put the necessary **punctuation marks, commas,** etc. into these sentences:

1. I owe you five farthings say the Bells of St Martins
2. Come in the Mayor cried looking bigger.
3. The actor recited The Knave of Hearts he stole some tarts
4. Youll never get away with it said the policeman Ill be watching you

TEST 24

I. Read very carefully through the following passage, and then answer the questions.

The Village School

The village school at that time provided all the instruction we were likely to ask for. It was a small stone barn divided by a wooden partition into two rooms—the Infants, the Big Ones. There was one dame teacher, and perhaps a younger girl assistant. Every child in the village crowding there remained until he was fourteen years old, then was presented to the working-field or factory with nothing in his head more burdensome than a few mnemonics, a jumbled list of wars, and a dreary image of the world's geography. It seemed enough to get by with, in any case; and was one up on our poor old grandparents.

The school, when I came to it, was at its peak. Universal education and unusual fertility had packed it to the walls with pupils. Wild boys and girls from miles around—from the outlying farms and half-hidden hovels way up at the ends of the valley—swept down each day to add to our numbers, bringing with them strange oaths and odours, quaint garments and curious pies.

Laurie Lee

1. How is the school building described? How had the two rooms been formed?
2. In one of the parts were the Infants. Who were the **Big Ones** in the other part?
3. Who did most of the teaching in the village school?
4. How do we know that it was the only school in a large area?
5. At what age did the children finally leave school?
6. What school lesson dealt with **a jumbled list of wars?**
7. A more than usual number of children had been born in the village. What two words tell us this?
8. Two kinds of after school jobs are named. What are they?
9. **Swept down each day.** Does this mean: (*a*) cleaned the school daily; (*b*) made their daily excursions to the school; (*c*) were brought in by the tide.
10. Find words or phrases that mean: elderly lady, dull picture, more than the grandparents had had, at its highest, swear

words, smells.
11. How do we know that there were no school dinners?

II. Colours. We use colours in everyday speech to denote certain conditions.

Example: To be in someone's **black books** means to be out of favour with them.

Explain the meanings of these colour connections:

1. He was the black sheep of the family.
2. March 11th is a red letter day for George.
3. They sent the orders in black and white.
4. Perhaps Mr Jenkins had blue blood in his veins.

III. Choose the correct **similes** from the following.

Example: If we wish to say someone or something is **bright** we say **as bright as a button.**

1. as pale as (*a*) death (*b*) a peach (*c*) a potato.
2. as green as (*a*) leaves (*b*) grass (*c*) the sea.
3. as deaf as (*a*) a post (*b*) a dodo (*c*) a roe.
4. as round as (*a*) a roundabout (*b*) a barrel (*c*) a robin.

IV. Write the following abbreviations in full:

1. He took law, became a **Q.C.**, worked for the **U.N.**, became a **V.I.P.**, and received the **O.M.**
2. From the **Y.H.A.** he moved to the **Y.M.C.A.** where his work won him an **O.B.E.**
3. When **H.M.S.** Lion sank, the **W.V.S.** looked after the survivors.
4. The poem might have been written by **Mme.** or **M.** Legrand.

V. Some words have a similar sound but are spelt differently. Choose the correct words from the brackets:

For (aught, ought) I know he is the (air, ere, heir) to the throne. I know that when the last monarch (dyed, died) it took six men to carry the (bier, beer) through the royal (borough, burrow).

TEST 25

I. Read very carefully through the following verses, and then answer the questions.

The Idlers

The gypsies lit their fires by the chalk-pit anew,
And the hoppled horses supped in the further dusk and dew;
The gnats flocked round the smoke like idlers as they were,
And through the goss and bushes the owls began to churr.

An elm above the woods the last of sunset glowed
With a dusky gold that filled the pond beside the road;
The cricketers had done, the leas all silent lay,
And the carrier's clattering wheels went past and died away.

The gypsies lolled and gossiped, and ate their stolen swedes,
Made merry with mouth-organs, worked toys with piths of reeds;
The old wives puffed their pipes, nigh as black as their hair,
And not one of them all seemed to know the name of care.

Edmund Blunden

1. Where did the gypsies light their fires?
2. Why were the horses **hoppled** (hobbled)? (*a*) to increase their pulling strength; (*b*) to stop them from straying; (*c*) to show which horse belonged to whom.
3. How do we know that evening was coming on?
4. How did the sunset seem to fill the pond?
5. What words tell us that the match was over?
6. The carrier had gone by. How does the poem tell us this?
7. How did the gypsies get their **swedes?**
8. What musical instrument did they play?
9. The gypsy women had a strange habit. What was it?
10. How do we know that the women were very happy and carefree?
11. Find words and phrases which mean: once again, the horses were having their evening meal, gorse, darkness was approaching, a deep, trilling sound, meadows, sat around lazily, talked about this and that, constructed toys from reeds.
12. Choose an alternative title for the poem: (*a*) Rustic joys; (*b*) Bowed down with grief and woe; (*c*) Working their fingers

to the bone.

II. Complete these **Car** words:

1. A house on wheels.
2. A small seed used for flavouring.
3. A short rifle.
4. A painful boil or pimple.
5. A dead body of an animal.
6. A cardboard case.
7. A fish.
8. A sweet-smelling flower.
9. A Christmas hymn.
10. A flesh-eating animal.

III. Find the **Odd Man Out** in these:

1. To order, to compel, to beg, to insist, to direct.
2. Footpad, burglar, warder, highwayman, bandit.
3. Cost, fee, charge, receipt, price.
4. Diligent, busy, indolent, industrious, zealous.
5. Bungling, awkward, adroit, clumsy, gawky.

IV. Write down this passage as it should be written, in verse. Begin each new line with a **capital letter.**

Not, Celia, that I juster am, or better than the rest, for I would change each hour like them, were not my heart at rest, but I am tied to very thee by every thought I have, thy face I only care to see, thy heart I only crave.

V. Two sentences can be joined together by using one word.

Example: That is the man. He stole my bicycle=That is the man **who** stole my bicycle.

Join the following sentences, you may have to alter some of them slightly. Choose from: **who, although, neither, which.**

1. He had no reply. He shouted many times.
2. Archie is not handsome. Dennis is not handsome.
3. The field was packed with people. They were all applauding excitedly.
4. You have tested the car. Father wants to buy it for us.

TEST 26

I. Read very carefully through the following passage, and then answer the questions.

The New Apprentice

Between Glass House Yard and Shoemaker's Row lies Friers Street, where Mr Paris's premises occupies a commanding position on the corner. In the gloom of the November evening his shop-window flares out extravagantly, as platoons of candles execute various dancing manoeuvres in flawless unison. On closer inspection, however, they turn out to be a single candle reflected in a cunning display of looking-glasses. Mr Paris is a master carver of mirror-frames; golden boys and golden grapes cluster round the silver mirrors and seem to invite, with dimpled arms outstretched, the passer-by to pause and contemplate himself.

Inside, in the dining-parlour, the family are sitting down to supper; Mr and Mrs Paris—a handsome couple who will be middle-aged when it suits them—Miss Lucinda, their young daughter, and Nightingale, the new apprentice. Nightingale has not long arrived. He has scarcely had time to wash himself before sitting down to table.

Leon Garfield

1. Was Mr Paris's shop in Glass House Yard, in Shoemaker's Row, or in Friers Street?
2. How do we know that it was well placed for all to see?
3. What was one of his favourite designs?
4. What effect did this design have on passers-by?
5. How did he make a single candle in the window do the work of so many?
6. What is the usual name for **dining-parlour**?
7. Mr and Mrs Paris will be middle-aged when it suits them. Does this mean: (*a*) they were not certain of their ages; (*b*) they had lost their birth certificates; (*c*) they did not feel middle-aged at that time.
8. Find words and phrases that mean: place of business; is very well lighted; great number of candles; when one examines more carefully; to look at himself.
9. From this list choose words or phrases that describe (*a*) Mr

Paris's business sense; artistic; talented; unskilled; imaginative; ordinary: (*b*) The Paris family: well-to-do; insufficient; hard up; refined; affluent; well-heeled.
10. When is someone called an apprentice?
11. Why did Nightingale scarcely have time to wash?

II. Rewrite the sentences below, filling each space with the correct word from this list: **with, to, of, from, off, for.**

1. He waited —— Peter to pack his case.
2. Susan was suffering —— chicken pox so she could not go.
3. The fog was so thick that the plane could not take ——.
4. According —— the weather forecast it should have been a lovely day.
5. The miserable old man strongly disagreed —— the broadcast.
6. He said that we were all victims —— a conspiracy.

III. Here are six famous quotations. Choose from the following list the people who said them: (*a*) Collectors during the Great Plague of London; (*b*) King Canute; (*c*) Winston Churchill; (*d*) Sir Francis Drake; (*e*) Richard III.

1. "A horse, a horse! My Kingdom for a horse!"
2. "We have time to finish the game and beat the Spaniards."
3. "Bring out your dead."
4. "I command the waves to go back."
5. "We shall fight on the beaches."

IV. Complete these **proverbs:**

1. Great minds ——
2. The early bird ——
3. Pride goes ——
4. Spare the rod ——

V. What or who do you associate with:

1. a library
2. a factory
3. a nursery
4. a reservoir
5. an apiary
6. a silo

TEST 27

I. Read very carefully through the following passage, and then answer the questions.

David Moss's Garden

David Moss lived with his family in the last house in Jubilee Row. Their house was like all the others, but their garden was something quite out of the ordinary; it ran straight back for the first twenty yards,- like all the other gardens; then, when the others stopped, this took a sudden turn to the right and, in another minute. it reached an unexpected destination. When the other gardens ended in a hedge, a fence, or a stretch of wire-netting, the Moss's garden was brought to a stop only by the softly flowing waters of the River Say.

"No, Becky, no!" said Mrs Moss. "You must never play by the river alone. David only goes on to the landing stage because he's older; if he falls in, he can swim."

The landing stage was over-grandly named, for nothing and nobody had ever landed there; it had been made by Mr Moss only so that he could more easily fill his water-can from the river.

A. Philippa Pearce

1. How was one boundary of the Moss's garden different from those of their neighbours?
2. What formed the end boundaries of the other gardens?
3. Which words tell us that the River Say was not a turbulent, hurrying river?
4. Why did Mrs Moss forbid Becky to play by the river alone? (*a*) because the girl's eyesight was not very good; (*b*) in case she should fall into the river and drown; (*c*) because she might not be able to find her way back to the house.
5. Why wasn't David forbidden?
6. Why was the landing-stage **over-grandly named?**
7. Why had Mr Moss built it?
8. Find words or phrases that mean: (*a*) identical; (*b*) unlike the others; (*c*) ended.
9. Why do you think David's street was called Jubilee Row?
10. Choose some suitable names for David's house.

II. From the three words inside the bracket, choose the one nearest in meaning to the word before the bracket.

Example: **Edge** (centre, margin, middle)   Answer: **margin**

1. **wretched**   (enraptured, miserable, blissful)
2. **assemble**   (gather, scatter, disperse)
3. **vigour**   (illness, healthiness, sickness)
4. **certain**   (doubtful, uncertain, positive)
5. **intention**   (choice, chance, fluke)

III. Arrange these words in **rhyming pairs**:

frozen, sou'wester, gaol, humming, Delhi, boatswain, goal, coming, Leicester, pale, whole, Nelly.

IV. From the words **Golf** and **Club** we can make the compound word **Golfclub**. Join the following fourteen words into pairs so as to make compound words: market, hearted, hammer, engine, lamp, water, home, sledge, oil, driver, drinking, sick, gardener, chicken.

V. Prefixes used before certain words change their meanings to **Not**.

Example: Clean—Unclean

Add the correct **prefix** from this list to each of these words so as to change the meaning. Use each prefix once. **in, un, non, dis, ir, im, ab, ig, il, mis.**

legal, regular, approve, sincere, behave, essential, normal, selfish noble, polite.

TEST 28

I. Read very carefully through the following passage, and then answer the questions.

The Young Soldier

There was a youthful private who listened with eager ears to the words of a tall soldier, and to the varied comments of his comrades. After receiving a full discussion concerning marches and attacks, he went to his hut and crawled through an intricate hole that served as a door. He wished to be alone with some new thoughts that had lately come to him.

He lay down on a wide bunk stretched across the end of the room. At the other end cracker boxes served as furniture from time to time, grouped about the fireplace. A folded tent was serving as a roof.

The youth was in a little trance of astonishment. So they were at last going to fight. On the morrow, perhaps, there would be a battle, and he would be in it. For a time he was obliged to labour to make himself believe. He could not accept, with assurance, an omen that he was about to mingle in one of those great affairs of the earth.

Stephen Crane

1. What words tell us that the man was a young man, and not an officer?
2. How had he spent much of his time in his early days as a soldier? (*a*) in fighting; (*b*) in listening to the talk of other soldiers; (*c*) in drinking and gambling.
3. What did the soldiers usually talk about?
4. Why did he suddenly wish to be alone? (*a*) he was tired; (*b*) he was shy; (*c*) he wanted to think things out.
5. Where did he go to be alone? What kind of bed was a **bunk**?
6. Besides the bunk, what other furniture was there?
7. What formed the roof?
8. The last paragraph is concerned with one of these: (*a*) at last he was going to fight; (*b*) that he was being transferred to another unit; (*c*) that the war would be over before he went into battle. Which of these?
9. Find words or phrases that mean: with close attention,

different remarks, he wanted to think, a difficult entrance, he could not easily believe, bewildered and mystified.
10. This is a story about the American Civil War. What names were given to the two sides which fought against each other?

II. From the **noun** Sorrow, we can make the **adjective** Sorrowful. Make an **adjective** from the **noun** in front of each sentence and use it to fill the space:

1. mountain   Nepal is a —— region.
2. meteor   Mohammed Ali had a —— rise to fame.
3. atmosphere   The weather is bringing —— problems to television enthusiasts.
4. arithmetic   Your pupil is an —— genius.
5. comfort   I don't think you'll find a —— chair here!
6. telescope   The camera was very expensive because it had a —— lens.

III. Rearrange each of these groups of letters to make **famous football teams:**

1. SLEECHA
2. CHORWIN
3. FROTDAW
4. TRONVEE
5. STOPREN
6. FLAMHU

IV. Write in full the **abbreviations** in the following sentences:

1. You can carry a **cello** on a **bus,** but not a **piano.**
2. She reached the **S.R.N.** grade, became a **SUPT.** and moved to **U.S.S.R.**
3. The **P.S.** in the letter said that the **Prof.** was a **Ph.D.**
4. They work out your **P.A.Y.E.** at **G.H.Q.**

V. Rearrange these six sentences from a story so that they appear in the correct order:

1. In they came from football or long walks.
2. A quarter-past-one bell now struck.
3. They went into the hall and took their places.
4. It began tolling for dinner.
5. Tom saw for the first time his future schoolfellows.
6. They brought with them pickles and sauce bottles.

TEST 29

I. Read very carefully through the following passage, and then answer the questions.

Good Queen Bess

Elizabeth I was Queen of England for forty-five years, from 1558 to 1603. During her reign many exciting things happened in our country and overseas. Sometimes we were in danger, as when Spain tried to conquer us.

Many famous Englishmen lived during the time Elizabeth was queen. There were heroes like Sir Francis Drake and Sir Walter Raleigh who went exploring in parts of the world that had not long been discovered. They returned to England with wonderful stories of happenings far away. They brought new plants from America, potatoes, tomatoes and tobacco; and also the first turkeys. English ships traded with India, Russia and remote countries where few foreigners had ever been.

Men who stayed at home also helped to make England a great country. It was once said that during Elizabeth's reign England became 'a nest of singing birds'. Men like William Shakespeare, Christopher Marlowe, and Edmund Spenser wrote splendid plays and poetry that will last for ever and ever.

1. For how long did Elizabeth I reign? In what century was most of her reign?
2. Which country threatened England during her reign?
3. Why are Drake and Raleigh amongst the great names of history?
4. What is meant by **England became 'a nest of singing birds'**? (*a*) they began importing birds from abroad; (*b*) our own birds improved their singing; (*c*) it was a description of our poets and playwrights.
5. What things were brought back to England that are now considered to be British?
6. What were the countries to the east which England began to trade with?
7. Why was Queen Elizabeth I nicknamed **Good Queen Bess?** (*a*) because she was a religious person; (*b*) she brought England safely through trying times; (*c*) because she was generous and

kind to all around her.
8. Find words or phrases that mean: seeking and finding, people from other countries, eternally.
9. Why did Elizabeth knight Drake and Raleigh?
10. Write down the name of a play or poem by Shakespeare, Marlowe and Spenser.

II. Rewrite these sentences in **plural** form:
1. The passer-by saw the hanger-on ignore the bye-law and break the curio.
2. The thief took the loaf from the shelf and cut it with a knife.
3. The cowboy with a lasso rode a bronco at the rodeo.
4. The cactus grew on a plateau, but sheep ate it.

III. Opposites. Write words **opposite** in meaning to those printed in heavy type, and complete the sentences:
1. Scrooge was **mean**, but became —— in the end.
2. The iron bar was **rigid**, but the wire was ——.
3. You must **inhale** and —— at equal speeds.
4. Glass is **transparent**; wood is ——.
5. The jury found the three men **guilty** of murder but found the woman ——.

IV. Write the following sports and pastimes in **alphabetical order:**

cricket, hockey, wrestling, water-polo, boxing, athletics, badminton, tennis, squash, golf, baseball, lacrosse, basketball, football, rugby.

V. Containers and their **contents.** Write these words in the correct, places in the paragraph below: **wardrobe, petrol, handbag, zoo, thermos-flask, trunk, tank, make-up, brief-case, carafe, tumbler, animals.**

He poured some wine from the —— into the ——, put the documents into his —— together with a —— of tea. She had taken clothes from her ——, enough to fill a ——. Her —— held her ——. They made sure the car's —— was full of ——. They sped past the —— where the —— were held captive.

TEST 30

I. Read very carefully through the following verses, and then answer the questions.

Spring

Spring, the sweet Spring, is the year's pleasant king;
Then blooms each thing, then maids dance in a ring;
Cold doth not sting, the pretty birds do sing,
   Cuckoo, jug-jug, pu-we, to-witta-woo.

The palm and may make country houses gay.
Lambs frisk and play, the shepherds pipe all day,
And we hear ay birds tune this merry lay,
   Cuckoo, jug-jug, pu-we, to-witta-woo.

The fields breathe sweet, the daisies kiss our feet,
Young lovers meet, old wives a-sunning sit,
In every street these tunes our ears do greet,
   Cuckoo, jug-jug, pu-we, to-twitta-woo!
   Spring! the sweet Spring!

Thomas Nash

1. **Cuckoo, jug-jug, pu-we, to-witta-woo.** What are these words meant to represent?
2. Spring **is the year's pleasant king.** What does this mean?
3. The **palm and may.** What do you think these are and how would they make houses gay?
4. **Shepherds pipe all day.** Does this mean: (*a*) they spend the time smoking; (*b*) they fill pails at the water pipe; (*c*) they play sweet music upon the pipes.
5. Why did Thomas Nash write **the daisies kiss our feet** not our shoes?
6. What was it that the fields were **breathing sweet?**
7. What words and phrases are used for: (*a*) give one an unpleasant shock; (*b*) a pleasant song.
8. 'In the Spring a young man's fancy lightly turns to thoughts of love.' How does Thomas Nash express this thought?
9. Choose an alternative title from these: (*a*) No time for fun and games; (*b*) Rural simplicity; (*c*) Urban hardships.

II. More about **colours** in everyday life. Complete these sentences using the correct **colour-words:**

1. He caught a —— Admiral butterfly.
2. She's too clever for me, quite a —— stocking.
3. He's thinking deeply. He's in a —— study.
4. They are about to sail. The —— Peter's hoisted.
5. He's got the plague, the dreaded —— Death.

III. Complete the following.

Example: **Man** is to **woman,** as **boy** is to . . .   Answer: **girl**

1. **Goals** are to **soccer** as **tries** are to ——.
2. **Huge** is to **tiny** as **Brobdingnagian** is to ——.
3. **Putt** is to **golf** as **pot** is to ——.
4. **Mountain** is to **valley** as **hill** is to ——.
5. **Nelson's Column** is to **London** as **Eiffel Tower** is to ——.

IV. Change these **direct speech** sentences into **indirect speech** sentences.

Example: "Be quiet," said the boy to his companion.   Answer: The boy told his companion to be quiet.

1. The boy came and said, "I'm sorry."
2. "I like the style of Jim's batting," said the coach.
3. Said Gorging Jack to Guzzling Jimmy, "I am extremely hungaree."
4. The shop assistant said, "This tea-set costs £25."

V. Use **single words** for the phrases printed below:

1. To leave one's native land and live abroad.
2. At this moment of time in this day and age.
3. The time at which the sun crosses the equator and day and night are equal.
4. Carefully and accurately expressed.

ACKNOWLEDGEMENTS

TEST 1 **After the Raid** from *The Machine Gunners* by Robert Westall. Macmillan London & Basingstoke;

TEST 2 **The Fisherman** from *The Old Man and the Sea* by Ernest Hemingway. Executors of the Ernest Hemingway Estate;

TEST 4 **The Feast at the Fjord** from *Vikings Dawn* by Henry Treece. Chapter 4 paras 1 and 2. The Children's Book Dept., of The Bodley Head;

TEST 6 **Trouble in the Darkness** from *The Night the Water Came* by Clive King. Kestrel and Puffin Books, Penguin Books Ltd.;

TEST 7 **Dantes Makes His Plans** from *The Count of Monte Cristo* by Alexandre Dumas;

TEST 8 **A Call to Arms** from *The Glass Knife* by John Tully. Methuen Children's Books Ltd.;

TEST 9 **The Music-making March Family** from *Little Women* by Louisa M. Alcott;

TEST 10 **I Promise You** from *The Woeful Lament of the Linen-Drapers Apprentice* by Haydn Perry. The Wayfarer Books III, Blackie & Son;

TEST 11 **The Dance Hall** from *Billy Liar* by Keith Waterhouse. Michael Joseph;

TEST 13 **In the Orchard** from *The Greengage Summer* by Rumer Godden. Macmillan London & Basingstoke;

TEST 14 **Captain Flint's Treasure** from *Treasure Island* by R. L. Stevenson;

TEST 15 **The Seed Shop** from *By Heart* memorable poems chosen by Sir Francis Maynell. Executors of the Muriel Stuart Estate;

TEST 16 **Space 1999. Mind-Breaks of Space** by Michael Butterworth and J. Jeff Jones. W. H. Allen & Co. Ltd.;

TEST 18 **Pop Larkins** from *When the Green Woods Laugh* by H. E. Bates. Laurence Pollinger and the Estate of the late H. E. Bates;

TEST 19 **The First Voyage of Sinbad the Sailor** from *The Arabian Nights Entertainments*;

TEST 20 *There Was An Indian* by J. C. Squire. Mr Raglan Squire;

TEST 21 **Finding a Lodge** from *Stalky & Co.* by Rudyard Kipling. A. P. Watt Ltd.;

TEST 23 **Deep in the Jungle** from *Westward Ho!* by Charles Kingsley;

TEST 24 **The Village School** from *Cider with Rosie* by Laurie Lee. The Hogarth Press;

TEST 25 *The Idlers* by Edmund Blunden. Reprinted by permission of A. D. Peters & Co. Ltd.;

TEST 26 **The New Apprentice** from *Mirror Mirror* by Leon Garfield. William Heinemann Ltd.;

TEST 27 **David Moss's Garden** from *Minnow on the Say* by A. Philippa Pearce. By permission of Oxford University Press;

TEST 28 **The Young Soldier** from *The Red Badge of Courage* by Stephen Crane.